Fragility and Conflict

Fragility and Conflict
On the Front Lines of the Fight against Poverty

Paul Corral, Alexander Irwin, Nandini Krishnan,
Daniel Gerszon Mahler, and Tara Vishwanath

 **WORLD BANK GROUP**

Contents

Boxes

Figures

Tables

Acknowledgments

This book was prepared by a team led by Tara Vishwanath. The core team included Paul Corral, Alexander Irwin, Nandini Krishnan, and Daniel Gerszon Mahler. The extended team included Ervin Dervisevic, Kadeem Khan, Anna Luisa Paffhausen, Utz Johann Pape, Lokendra Phadera, and Rakesh Gupta Nichanametla Ramasubbaiah, all of whom provided key inputs.

The work has been carried out under the general direction of Carolina Sánchez-Páramo and Benu Bidani. The team is also grateful for guidance and advice from the Fragility, Conflict and Violence Group, especially, Franck Bousquet, Xavier Devictor, and Caroline Bahnson.

Elizabeth Howton and Venkat Gopalakrishnan led the communication and messaging of the book, with inputs from Paul Gallagher and Victoria Smith. Others who helped support this book include Miguel Angel De Corral Martin, Maria Davalos, Diego Chaves Gonzalez, Samuel Freije-Rodriguez, Carolina Mejia-Mantilla, Ambar Narayan, Umar Serajuddin, Dhiraj Sharma, Emi Suzuki, and Judy Yang. Special thanks are also due to Sharad Alan Tandon for his inputs related to 2016 Gallup Poll analysis.

The team gratefully acknowledges advice from the peer reviewers Xavier Devictor, Dean Jolliffe, and Luis-Felipe Lopez-Calva. The team also appreciates the many helpful comments from Maurizio Bussolo, Louise Cord, Sascha Djumena, Pablo Fajnzylber, Roberta Gatti, and Lucia Hanmer. In addition, the team gratefully acknowledges help from the many people who have commented on various drafts of the chapters, as well as from those who have provided assistance in the preparation of this book. Finally, this book would not have been possible without the hard work and dedication of the thousands of enumerators and survey respondents around the world who have graciously shared the details of their lives and the many facets of poverty.

About the Authors

Paul Corral is a senior economist in the Office of the HD Chief Economist. He previously worked as a data scientist with the Poverty and Equity Global Practice, where he focused on small area estimation methods and applications. He has published peer-reviewed articles on agriculture and development for specific African countries and is the author of multiple Stata commands. He holds a PhD in economics from American University and an MSc degree in agricultural economics from the University of Hohenheim.

Alexander Irwin, MD, PhD, is an independent global health writer and researcher living in Hong Kong SAR, China, and in New York. He has held staff and faculty appointments at the World Health Organization, the Harvard FXB Center for Health and Human Rights, and the World Bank. He has contributed to recent global reports on tobacco control policy, antimicrobial resistance, and health financing in low- and middle-income countries.

Nandini Krishnan is a senior economist with the Poverty and Equity Global Practice of the World Bank. She leads the poverty program in Afghanistan and co-leads the poverty program in Bangladesh. She has worked on many fragile and conflict-affected situations (including Iraq, the West Bank and Gaza, and the Republic of Yemen) and co-led analytical programs focusing on refugee hosting situations. She has supported impact evaluations of large-scale projects and programs in Nigeria, South Africa, and Tanzania, and holds a PhD in economics from Boston University.

Daniel Gerszon Mahler is a Young Professional in the Development Data Group, where he is part of the Sustainable Development Statistics team. Previously he was with the Poverty and Equity Global Practice, where he contributed to the practice's global agenda on measuring poverty and inequality. Prior to joining the World Bank, he was a visiting fellow at Harvard University's Department of Government and worked for the Danish Ministry of Foreign Affairs. Daniel holds a PhD in economics from the University of Copenhagen.

Tara Vishwanath is a lead economist and a global lead of the Welfare Implications of Climate, Fragility, and Conflict Risks Global Solutions Group in the Poverty and Equity Practice of the World Bank. Prior to joining the Africa Region, she led the poverty program in the Middle East and North Africa and the South Asia regions. Before joining the World Bank, she was a professor in the department of economics at Northwestern University. She has published widely in leading international economics journals spanning research topics in economic theory, labor economics, and development. She holds a bachelor's degree in physics and statistics and a PhD in economics from Cornell University.

Abbreviations

ACLED	Armed Conflict Location and Event Data Project
CPIA	Country Policy and Institutional Assessment
DHS	Demographic and Health Surveys
FCS	fragile and conflict-affected situations
GDP	gross domestic product
GPS	global positioning system
HCI	Human Capital Index
HFCE	household final consumption expenditure
IDP	internally displaced person
OECD	Organisation for Economic Co-operation and Development
PCA	principal components analysis
PPP	purchasing power parity
UCDP	Uppsala Conflict Data Program
UNHCR	United Nations High Commissioner for Refugees

Introduction

Under Sustainable Development Goal 1, all countries have pledged to end extreme poverty by 2030. This book examines what are likely to be the most intractable barriers to reaching that goal: conflict and state fragility.

The book addresses policy makers and their technical teams, global and national development practitioners, advocates, and all those with a stake in stopping extreme poverty from disfiguring human lives. The book aims to show why addressing fragility and conflict is critical for poverty goals. It presents new estimates of welfare in economies in fragile and conflict-affected situations (FCS), filling gaps in previous knowledge, and analyzes the multidimensional nature of poverty in these settings. It discusses the long-term consequences of conflict and introduces a data-driven classification of countries by fragility profile, showing opportunities for tailored policy interventions and the need for monitoring different markers of fragility.

The book delivers five key messages:

- Extreme poverty is increasingly concentrated in FCS, and global poverty goals will not be met without intensified action there.
- Data deprivation affects 70 percent of people in FCS and represents a major barrier to understanding and addressing their welfare needs.
- Poverty in FCS typically involves simultaneous deprivations in multiple dimensions, and intervention strategies must also act through multiple channels.
- Conflict compromises development by damaging human capital and productivity, with effects that last for generations.
- Clustering countries by fragility profile reveals two important findings. First, there is significant heterogeneity within FCS countries, calling for a differentiated policy and programming approach for more effective solutions. Second, there are important markers of fragility, in both FCS and non-FCS countries, that need to be monitored for preventive action.

An Urgent Challenge—and a Window to Respond

It has long been known that economies in FCS suffer high poverty rates and have difficulty reducing them. But the implications of FCS for ending global poverty have grown more urgent as conflict and fragility themselves have changed—with conflict less tied to confrontations between national armies, and often more devastating to civilian populations. Since World War II, interstate conflict has fallen sharply, but intrastate conflicts and interpersonal violence have risen (von Einsiedel et al. 2017). Despite fewer wars between nations, global safety and security indicators have deteriorated over the past decade (Institute for Economics and Peace 2019). The number of forcibly displaced people worldwide is at its highest point since World War II (UNHCR 2019).

While rates of extreme poverty have fallen rapidly in many countries since 2000, this does not apply to countries in conflict. In many FCS, poverty rates appear to be rising, stagnating, or at best declining slowly. And the conditions of FCS are spreading, casting their shadow over a growing number of countries and an increasing share of the global population. The number of people living in close proximity to conflict zones has more than doubled in the past decade, driven by wars in the Syrian Arab Republic and the Republic of Yemen that alone affected millions of people. If current demographic trends continue, by the end of 2020 the majority of the world's extremely poor people will live in FCS.

This means that ending extreme poverty requires accelerating gains where poverty has been most intractable: in FCS and Sub-Saharan Africa. By definition, the economies concerned are often characterized by weak institutions and political instability. They require significant reforms to policy and delivery mechanisms along multiple dimensions to achieve growth and poverty reduction. In turn, better policies depend on reliable data, which many of these countries lack.

With extreme poverty in FCS poised to overtake that in all other settings combined, the world has a critical window in which to confront this threat. Ultimately, support to conflict-affected countries needs to be tailored, innovative, and focused on the drivers of fragility and factors of resilience. Policy aims must include, but go beyond, economic growth and poverty reduction to promote peace and stability. But what strategies can advance these aims, and how can countries measure progress?

Ultimately, answering these questions will require better understanding the causes of conflict. That inquiry lies beyond the scope of this book, however. Recent research has enriched understanding of conflict's causal mechanisms at a theoretical level. Yet comparatively little progress has been made in empirical work to disentangle specific risks or mechanisms that lead to conflict or fragility. The literature is replete with cross-country analyses, but with no consensus on how far they provide sound evidence of causal relations. Recent country-specific studies have shed fresh light by analyzing, for example, climate-related or economic shocks as potential causal factors in some conflicts. Despite advances, however, research has yet to systematically map drivers of fragility and conflict in a way that can support targeted prevention. More work in this area is urgently needed.[1]

In light of these challenges, this book does not try to elucidate conflict's causes. Rather, it documents the welfare effects of fragility and conflict, to some extent taking fragility and conflict conditions as a given. Within these limits, the book seeks to disentangle select key issues, clarify impacts on human welfare and countries' economic prospects, and propose tools that can inform policy responses tailored to country contexts.

Book Structure

Chapter 1 of the book makes the case that the fight against poverty will not be won without addressing fragility and conflict. It shows that, while the world has made impressive progress in poverty reduction in the past 20 years, the global prevalence of conflict has worsened, and extreme poverty is increasingly concentrated in FCS. The chapter discusses how the lack of reliable data on poverty and welfare in FCS hampers monitoring and action, and it suggests how data gaps can be overcome. Improved assumptions on poverty in FCS lead to higher estimates of the number of extremely poor people in the world.

Poor people in FCS face challenges that go far beyond monetary poverty. Chapter 2 analyzes these multiple welfare shortfalls, which often include lack of basic infrastructure and inability to access quality education and health care. The section marshals data showing that poor people in FCS are substantially more likely than the poor elsewhere to experience multiple forms of deprivation simultaneously.

Chapter 3 examines the long-term consequences of conflict and fragility. Reviewing the literature with a human-capital lens, the analysis suggests that conflict's negative effects can be worse and longer-lasting than is commonly understood. Health and educational outcomes are compromised, not only among people who experience conflict as children, but also among the children of those original victims, threatening productivity and economic growth across generations.

How should countries and the development community meet these challenges? Chapter 4 uses a data-driven approach to identify distinct groups of economies with similar fragility profiles. Such analyses make a strong case for risk monitoring, early action, and a differentiated policy and programming approach. These and other implications for learning and action to effectively address extreme poverty in FCS are further explored in chapter 5, which presents the book's conclusions.

Note

1. This unfinished agenda also implies the need to improve data collection that can test recent theory on factors such as grievances and mistrust. More nuanced information on governance at subnational levels can also be harnessed to test theories of conflict through empirical research.

References

Institute for Economics and Peace. 2019. *Global Peace Index 2019: Measuring Peace in a Complex World*. Sydney: Institute for Economics and Peace. http://visionofhumanity.org/reports.

UNHCR (United Nations High Commissioner for Refugees). 2019. *Global Trends: Forced Displacement in 2018*. Geneva: UNHCR.

von Einsiedel, Sebastian, Louise Bosetti, James Cockayne, Cale Salih, and Wilfred Wan. 2017. "Civil War Trends and the Changing Nature of Armed Conflict." Occasional Paper 10, United Nations University, Tokyo.

1. Fragility, Conflict, and Extreme Poverty

Key Messages

- *The number of people living in proximity to conflict has doubled since 2007, and one in five people in the Middle East and North Africa now live in such circumstances.*
- *Five-hundred million people live in economies in fragile and conflict-affected situations (FCS) for which there are no or outdated data on poverty.*
- *Accounting for the missing data adds more than 30 million people to the global poverty count. Of these, 17 million additional poor are in FCS, resulting in a 7 percent increase in the number of poor in FCS.*
- *The 43 economies in the world with the highest poverty rates are in FCS and/or in Sub-Saharan Africa.*
- *More than half of the world's poor will be living in FCS by the end of 2020.*

Background: Living and Dying in a Two-Speed World

Extreme poverty has decreased rapidly in recent decades, an unprecedented human achievement. Between 1990 and 2015, countries' successful development strategies reduced the proportion of the global population living in extreme poverty from 36 to 10 percent (World Bank 2018).[1] Over the same period, the number of people in extreme poverty fell by more than a billion.

Yet significant bastions of poverty persist, increasingly related to FCS.[2] The world's success in driving down extreme poverty is complicated by the failure to reduce FCS. Of deep concern is that the prevalence of FCS is on the rise today. Old conflicts remain unresolved, while new ones continue to erupt. As a result, the number of people living in proximity to conflict—formally, within 60 kilometers of at least 25 conflict-related deaths—has risen steadily and doubled in the past 10 years (figure 1.1; and see appendix A). At the same time, the number of forcibly displaced people worldwide has more than doubled, exceeding 70 million in 2017, the highest figure in decades (figure 1.2).

These trends of increasing violence and conflict particularly affect the Middle East and North Africa region. There, in 2017, one in five persons lived in close proximity to a major conflict event (appendix A). This is propelled by the ongoing conflicts in Syria

FIGURE 1.1 **The World's Population Living in Proximity to Conflict Deaths Has Doubled in 10 Years**

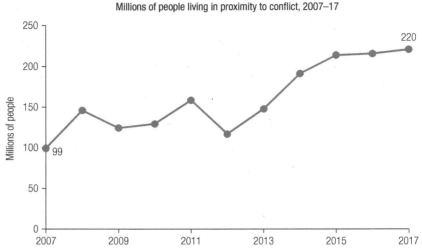

Millions of people living in proximity to conflict, 2007–17

Sources: UCDP 2019; LandScan 2012.

Note: The figure shows the world's population living within 60 kilometers of a major conflict event, defined as 25 or more battle-related deaths in the year in question. In relative terms, the share of the world's population living in close proximity to conflict has increased from 1.5 percent in 2007 to 3.0 percent in 2017.

FIGURE 1.2 **The Number of Displaced People Is on the Rise**

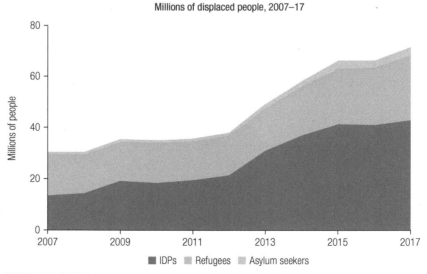

Millions of displaced people, 2007–17

Sources: UNHCR 2019; IDMC 2019.

Note: IDPs = internally displaced persons.

and the Republic of Yemen, where more than half of the population—84 percent and 51 percent, respectively—lived in close proximity to conflict.

A two-speed world is emerging, sharply demarcated by conflict. On one side, economies free of FCS have strongly reduced extreme poverty, paving the way for additional development progress. On the other, economies affected by FCS confront intractable poverty and faltering growth, with development targets slipping out of reach. In the decades ahead, as economies not plagued by conflict and institutional fragility likely continue to climb the development ladder, global poverty will increasingly be concentrated in economies in FCS. To end extreme poverty by 2030, as pledged under the first Sustainable Development Goal, the global community must focus on economies in FCS.

While extreme poverty is increasingly linked to fragility and conflict, due to insecurity and lack of institutional capacity, accurately measuring poverty in economies in FCS is challenging. This deprivation of data makes it difficult to create a truly global picture of fragility, poverty, and their interactions. The lack of data also prevents evaluating the success of policies aimed to reduce poverty in economies in FCS. Without evaluation of policies, it is challenging for decision makers to prioritize new investments by directing resources to programs that work and to the places most in need of attention.

The remainder of this chapter discusses the data challenges connected with poverty in FCS, suggests how data shortfalls may be overcome, and explores what doing so means for the global fight against poverty.

Data Deprivation in FCS

More than 1,000 estimates of international poverty spanning more than 150 economies have been conducted over the past 20 years (PovcalNet). These estimates are based on carefully planned household surveys, which contain a measure of the value of household consumption or income for the sampled households. To inform discussions about national poverty, the surveys must be nationally representative, which requires the ability to get to all parts of an economy. This is challenging for economies where parts of the territory are plagued by conflict and violence, as concern for the safety of enumerators inhibits survey implementation in the unsafe regions.

Even if conflict does not prohibit fielding nationally representative surveys, facilitating internationally comparable poverty estimates also requires auxiliary data, which can be difficult to obtain in settings of institutional fragility. To compare poverty rates in a country obtained at different points in time, consumer price indices are used to ensure that all consumption aggregates are expressed in the same price level. When comparing poverty rates across countries, local currencies are converted using purchasing power parity exchange rates to account for differences in the purchasing power across countries, ensuring that a dollar can purchase the same bundle of goods and services in the different settings compared. Such price statistics do not come out of the blue but require their own surveys and a minimal level of statistical capacity in an economy. Ensuring such a level of statistical capacity can be challenging for economies facing high institutional fragility, further hindering economies in FCS from delivering international poverty estimates. Some economies with low technical capacity have obtained the necessary data, but data quality was not deemed adequate for international poverty estimates to be computed.

The institutional and safety conditions necessary to generate international poverty estimates imply that many economies plagued by fragility, conflict, and violence have no or only outdated estimates of the living standards of their populations.[3] To characterize a situation of inadequate poverty-related data, economies are referred to as *data deprived*. Economies are considered data deprived if they do not have international poverty estimates within two years of 2015, the latest year for which global poverty numbers are expressed.

Data deprivation on poverty in economies in FCS takes multiple forms (figure 1.3). The most severe occurs in economies that have no international poverty estimates at all. In 2015, this concerned the population of economies comprising 74 million people, including economies that have been subject to prolonged situations of conflict and/or institutional fragility, such as Eritrea and Somalia.

A second type of data deprivation exists in economies that have international poverty estimates but where there is reason to believe that these might be outdated. Although this kind of deprivation also occurs for economies not affected by conflict and violence, it is magnified in cases of conflict. For an economy that is not undergoing significant changes, poverty estimates that are a couple of years out of date might still contain a strong signal about the living standards of the population. But three-year-old poverty estimates for an economy that has meanwhile fallen into a civil war are of little value. Likewise, poverty estimates for economies that, since their last survey, managed to escape conflict or saw existing conflict spread may not reveal much about those economies' current living standards. Economies containing around 400 million people suffer from these sorts of data deprivation. This includes economies such as Mali and Syria, where the latest international poverty estimates currently available predate the start of a conflict.

Finally, worldwide there is very little poverty data for displaced people. Although displaced people may live in economies that have recent data, they are often not accounted for in household surveys, since individuals living in camps are not part of the sampling frame.[4] With the number of displaced people worldwide on the rise and global poverty rates steadily declining, this is increasingly relevant for generating accurate international estimates of poverty (World Bank 2018). Displaced people are likely to have higher poverty rates, since they face weak labor demand, may have been subject

FIGURE 1.3 Patterns of International Poverty Data Deprivation in FCS

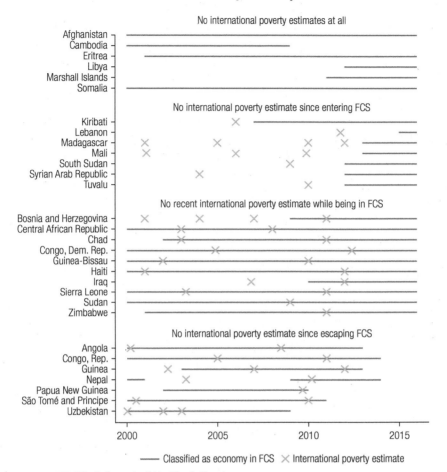

Sources: PovcalNet; World Bank, Harmonized List of Fragile Situations.

Note: The figure shows economies that are data deprived with respect to international poverty estimates, due to FCS. Data deprivation is defined as not having international poverty estimates within two years of 2015, which is the latest year for which global poverty estimates are expressed as of November 2019. Years in which international poverty estimates were produced in the economies listed are indicated by an X. Some of the listed economies might have *national* poverty estimates but lack credible purchasing power parity exchange rates, or they might have international poverty estimates that are not deemed satisfactory for international poverty comparisons. Others might have generated international poverty estimates after 2017 or may obtain international poverty estimates within two years of 2015 in the future. FCS = fragile and conflict-affected situations.

to psychological distress, and too often lack access to basic infrastructure services (Beegle and Christiaensen 2019).

All told, these different forms of data deprivation affect economies in FCS where more than half a billion people reside. This constitutes 71 percent of all individuals living in economies in FCS. Thus, for seven out of ten people in economies affected by conflict or fragility, our knowledge of how they are faring by international poverty standards is limited or nonexistent.[5] Data deprivations exist in other parts of the world as well, but only three in ten individuals outside of FCS live in economies that were data deprived in 2015.

Overcoming Data Deprivation

To tackle or work around these critical data shortages and generate timely international poverty estimates for all economies of the world, statistical assumptions and imputations are necessary. The main techniques used in this book and their underlying assumptions are briefly summarized in box 1.1 and discussed in detail in appendix B. Although these assumptions are imperfect, they are necessary to determine whether poverty rates are higher in economies plagued by fragility, conflict, and violence, and to calculate the share of the global poor living in economies in FCS.

Assumptions Made to Overcome Data Deprivations

Economies with no international poverty estimates

For economies that lack any international poverty estimates whatsoever, data on gross domestic product (GDP) per capita in purchasing power terms are used to predict poverty rates. This approach starts with data on international poverty and GDP per capita from economies that report both and uses these data to generate a relationship between the two variables. Poverty rates can subsequently be predicted from GDP per capita alone. For economies that also lack estimates of GDP per capita in purchasing power terms, satellite imagery of nighttime lighting is used to first infer levels of GDP per capita. Satellite nightlight imagery has been shown to be highly predictive of GDP per capita and human development in past analyses (Bruederle and Hodler 2018; Henderson, Vernon, and Weil 2012; Pinkovskiy and Sala-i-Martin 2016).

Countries lacking recent poverty data

For economies where some poverty data exist, but they are outdated, the World Bank generally assumes that the growth (or shrinkage) in GDP per capita (or household final consumption expenditure) registered since the country's last poverty estimate is fully passed through to the consumption vector that is measured in household surveys (Prydz et al. 2019). Poverty is then estimated using this adjusted consumption vector. This assumption holds rather well for economies not in FCS but, as shown in appendix B, it does not hold well for economies in FCS. For economies that erupt into conflict or escape conflict, evidence suggests that only half of growth in GDP per capita is passed through to the welfare observed in household surveys. This implies that, when an economy experiences conflict, violence, or fragility, GDP per capita moves more than does welfare. Here, this pattern is accounted for by assuming that only half of growth in GDP per capita is passed through to welfare observed in household surveys. Under this assumption,

(Box continues on the following page.)

Fragility and Conflict

Assumptions Made to Overcome Data Deprivations *(continued)*

poverty rates can be generated for economies that have outdated poverty data, as long as those economies have data on growth in GDP per capita in the period since their last reliable poverty measurement.

Poverty among displaced people

Many displaced people are not captured in household surveys. To the extent that they have higher poverty rates than their nondisplaced counterparts, this could matter for global poverty counts. To alleviate this problem, a small number of country-level studies are used to get a sense of what poverty is like for displaced populations. Studies from five economies spanning three continents jointly suggest that displaced populations have roughly the same distribution of consumption as neighboring nondisplaced communities, but that consumption among displaced people is reduced by about 25 percent across the board. This assumption is used to adjust national poverty rates based on their share of displaced people. As discussed in detail in appendix B, this could yield a slight overestimation of poverty rates, since many displaced people not living in camps may be captured in household surveys.

The assumptions are intended for global analysis of poverty, and, to be sure, better assumptions can and should be made to generate poverty estimates at the national level for data-deprived economies suffering from FCS. More tailored strategies have recently been deployed to overcome data deprivation concerning high-poverty economies in FCS. The strategy used in Somalia is a prominent example of how innovative methods can be used at the country level to deliver credible estimates of poverty in countries suffering from weak institutions and conflict (box 1.2). To ensure that all economies have an estimate of poverty while keeping the methodology transparent and tractable, the simpler methods discussed in box 1.1 are used in this book.

Tackling Data Deprivation at the Country Level: Lessons from Somalia

Contributed by Utz Johann Pape

For decades, Somalia has been a fragile country loaded with a heavy debt burden. Because of its multiple challenges, Somalia provides a valuable laboratory for testing how to overcome data deprivations with innovative solutions that may apply across a range of economies in FCS.

In 2017, to apply for debt forgiveness under the Heavily Indebted Poor Countries initiative, Somalia needed to prepare an Interim Poverty Reduction Strategy Paper describing

(Box continues on the following page.)

BOX 1.2

Tackling Data Deprivation at Country Level: Lessons from Somalia
(continued)

poverty in the country and deriving priority actions to monitor and reduce it. However, no poverty data were available for Somalia since the collapse of Siad Barre's regime in 1991. To fill the gap, the World Bank—together with Somali authorities—implemented a household survey to estimate poverty in this still-fragile country grappling with an array of complex challenges.

Somalia's most recent census had been conducted in 1987—seriously outdated, particularly in light of the country's experience of large-scale migration and displacement. Even though a population estimation survey was implemented in 2014 by the United Nations Population Fund, no rural enumeration area maps were available. Given the financial, logistical, and security challenges to demarcate enumeration areas in Somalia in a reasonable lapse of time, satellite images were used to estimate population density across Somalia to allow automatic demarcation of enumeration areas with manual refinements. The resulting enumeration area maps were then used as a sampling frame for the household surveys and are now available from the Somali statistical authorities for new surveys.

Tight security requirements prompted further innovations to minimize the time enumerators would spend in the field. First, a segmenting approach was used for sampling to avoid lengthy listings of enumeration areas. Enumeration areas were partitioned based on satellite images in small segments so that an enumerator would be able to list all dwellings from a central point in the segment. Second, the questionnaire design was adjusted by the rapid consumption methodology to minimize time needed to measure consumption. Instead of going through the full list of consumption items with all households, key consumption items were assigned to a core module, while the remaining items were split into four optional modules. Each household reported only on the core module and one of the optional modules. The systematically missing information was then statistically imputed after field work. Third, implementation logistics were optimized for a minimal footprint in the field without quality deterioration. To achieve this, remote monitoring and management of tablet and phone software were introduced, as well as global positioning system (GPS) geofencing to ensure that enumerators conducting interviews in assigned areas paired with near-real-time data quality monitoring and feedback cycles. Fourth, geospatial information helped to impute poverty estimates to a few no-go areas.

With the help of the new methodology, World Bank and government partners were able to estimate that poverty in Somalia was 70 percent in 2017 (figure B1.2.1). Poverty is widespread and deep, particularly among rural residents, internally displaced persons (IDPs), and children. While there are better conditions in cities, urban populations still struggle with a high poverty rate of 64 percent. Shocks like the recent drought have severe impacts on livelihoods, as safety nets are largely informal, often relying on remittances, and generally inadequate. Safety nets are not available to specific vulnerable groups such as IDPs.

(Box continues on the following page.)

BOX 1.2

Tackling Data Deprivation at Country Level: Lessons from Somalia (*continued*)

While the country's problems remain daunting, creative strategies to solve critical data shortfalls will be pivotal in enabling Somalia to end cycles of violence and advance toward a better future.

FIGURE B1.2.1   Poverty across Population Groups in Somalia, 2017

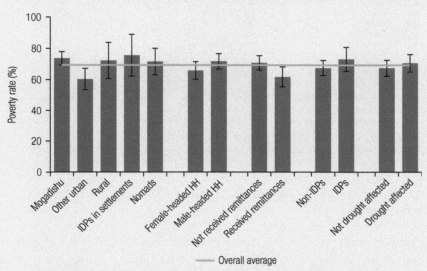

Sources: Himelein et al. 2017; Pape and Mistiaen 2018; Pape and Wollburg 2019; World Bank 2019.
Note: HH = household; IDPs = internally displaced persons.

A Clearer Picture of Global Poverty

With data deprivations in FCS accounted for, international poverty estimates can be derived for all economies in the world. Such estimates reveal a demarcated planet, with high levels of poverty in economies in Sub-Saharan Africa and economies in FCS, and lower levels elsewhere. Based on 2019 nowcasts of poverty in all economies (see box 1.3 for a discussion of how these nowcasts are derived), the 43 economies in the world with the highest poverty rate are either in FCS or in Sub-Saharan Africa—and of these 43, more than a third fall into both categories (figure 1.4). All of these economies are predicted to have poverty rates of 19 percent or higher. In contrast, all economies that are neither in Sub-Saharan Africa nor in FCS are predicted to have poverty rates below 19 percent.

FIGURE 1.4   The 43 Economies with the Highest Poverty Rates Are All in FCS and/or in Sub-Saharan Africa

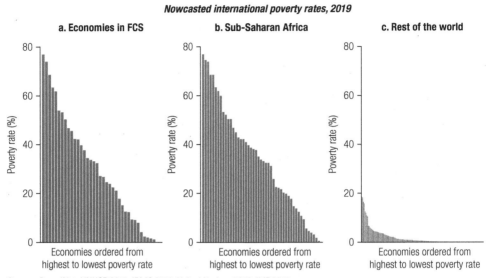

Nowcasted international poverty rates, 2019

a. Economies in FCS

b. Sub-Saharan Africa

c. Rest of the world

Economies ordered from highest to lowest poverty rate

Economies ordered from highest to lowest poverty rate

Economies ordered from highest to lowest poverty rate

Sources: PovcalNet; UNHCR 2019; IDMC 2019; United Nations 2019; IMF 2019.
Note: 19 economies are both in Sub-Saharan Africa and classified as FCS. FCS = fragile and conflict-affected situations.

Better Analysis in FCS Shows that Global Poverty Has Been Underestimated

These country-level estimates of poverty rates can be compiled to get a better understanding of what global poverty looks like, while accounting for the data deprivations in situations of fragility. The latest global poverty estimate, for 2015, indicates that 10 percent of the global population lives in extreme poverty. This figure, however, does not explicitly account for poverty in FCS economies without data. It assumes that FCS economies without data are as poor as the regions they belong to, which is often too positive an assumption. Nor does this estimate take fully into account that displaced people tend to be poorer than the nondisplaced population, or that outdated data in situations of FCS perhaps ought to be extrapolated differently.

Adjusting for these forms of data deprivation raises the global poverty rate by 0.5 percentage points (figure 1.5a). Although this might seem minor, the correction signifies that 33 million more people are living in extreme poverty than had previously been understood (figure 1.5b). Of these 33 million, 17 million additional poor are in FCS, resulting in a 7 percent increase in the number of poor in FCS. The added poor primarily emerge through better estimates of poverty in economies without data. Recently, however, with the surge in IDPs, better estimates of poverty among this population group have also contributed to revealing the undercount. With poverty declining in economies not in FCS, it is likely that the share of poor in FCS added due to better assumptions will increase further in the coming years.

Fragility and Conflict

FIGURE 1.5 Impacts of Better Assumptions about Individuals Affected by Conflict

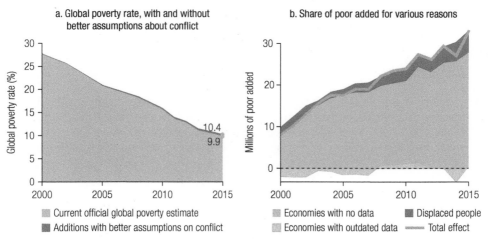

a. Global poverty rate, with and without better assumptions about conflict

b. Share of poor added for various reasons

Current official global poverty estimate

Additions with better assumptions on conflict

Economies with no data

Economies with outdated data

Displaced people

Total effect

Sources: PovcalNet; UNHCR 2019; IDMC 2019; IMF 2019; United Nations 2019.

Note: Panel a: The 2015 official estimate of global poverty without special assumptions for FCS (9.93 percent) differs slightly from the 2015 official estimate that can be found in PovcalNet as of November 2019 (9.98 percent). This is because the 9.93 version uses more recent population data. Panel b: The total effect shows the sum of the three components. Accounting for outdated data sometimes *reduces* the number of poor. This happens when economies in conflict diminish their GDP per capita after the last survey point. The adjustments made here assume that only part of this drop in GDP per capita is passed through to welfare observed in household surveys, thereby yielding a slightly lower poverty rate than estimated using the conventional method.

Poverty Rates Have Risen in FCS, as They Fall Elsewhere

With conflict on the rise, and the addition of 33 million poor people to the global poverty count due to situations of fragility, conflict, and violence, it is worthwhile to ask how poverty within economies suffering from FCS has evolved over time. Analyzing this is challenging due to the shifting group of economies that fall into this category. Although the annual Harmonized List of Fragile Situations could be used to that end, a change in the methodology makes it difficult to make comparisons over time. To circumvent this issue, the classification criteria behind the current list are used retrospectively to establish, for a past year, which economies would have been classified as in FCS by today's standards. We refer to the outcome as the *backcasted* FCS list. More details on this methodology are presented in box 1.3 and visually in appendix C.

With this backcasted methodology, poverty trends can be assessed. Since 2000, the poverty rate in economies not in FCS has steadily declined, from 26 percent to an estimated 5 percent in 2019 (figure 1.6a). Projections based on forecasted growth rates suggest that this decline will continue, and by 2030, economies not in FCS will have a poverty rate of 2.4 percent. This is well below the target of 3 percent the World Bank Group has set as one of its twin goals to achieve globally by 2030. In other words, if we ignore economies in FCS, the world is on track to nearly eliminate extreme poverty within a decade.

Backcasting and Forecasting FCS and Poverty

Backcasting FCS

In order to analyze the change in poverty in economies in FCS over time, the same definition of status as FCS should be applied throughout. The World Bank's Harmonized List of Fragile Situations (World Bank 2018) has recently undergone methodological changes that require adjustments to ensure comparability across time. For the analysis in this subsection, the classification criteria used for the 2019–20 list are applied retrospectively. These criteria rely on multiple data sources: (a) data on conflict deaths from the Armed Conflict Location and Event Data Project; (b) data on conflict deaths from the Uppsala Conflict Data Program; (c) data on Country Policy and Institutional Assessment scores from the World Bank, African Development Bank, and Asian Development Bank; (d) data on the presence of United Nations peacekeeping operations; and (e) data on refugees from the United Nations High Commissioner for Refugees. A visual representation of these classification criteria is presented in appendix C.

Forecasting FCS

It is not possible to know which economies will be in FCS in the coming years, yet this is needed to look at poverty trends toward 2030. The present analysis calculates poverty in FCS assuming that all economies currently in FCS remain that way until 2030, while no additional economies join the group. This should be seen, not as a prediction, but rather as the hypothetical outcome if this scenario were to prevail. The economies assumed to be in FCS going forward matter greatly for the forecasted share of poor in FCS (Jolliffe et al. 2014). Assumptions are also needed about the size of the displaced population in each country, which likewise cannot be known in advance. Here, it is assumed that the displaced population within each economy grows in size in accordance with the rest of the population.

Backcasting poverty

Estimates of poverty going back to 2000 are from PovcalNet, with adjustments for missing data in FCS as discussed in box 1.1.

Forecasting poverty rates

The latest global poverty estimates from PovcalNet are for the year 2015. To get a sense of how poverty has evolved since then, and how poverty is likely to evolve toward 2030, nowcasting and forecasting methods are applied. To nowcast country-level poverty rates to 2019 for economies not in FCS, it is assumed that the growth observed in GDP per capita between 2015 and 2019 (or since the latest survey, if later than 2015) is passed through in a distribution-neutral manner to the welfare vector. For economies in FCS, it is assumed that only 50 percent of the growth is passed through, based on the discussion in appendix B. A similar method is applied from 2019 to 2030, but instead of using observed growth rates in GDP per capita, projected growth rates in GDP per capita from the IMF's World Economic Outlook are used.

This picture changes dramatically when looking at economies in FCS. These economies have always been poorer than their counterparts, but, more worrisome, their poverty rate has increased from about 22 percent in 2012 to an estimated 37 percent in 2019 (figure 1.6a). The change in the average poverty rate in economies in FCS is largely driven by the composition of economies that are in FCS. The rise from 2012 to 2019 is mainly spurred by Nigeria entering FCS status in this period, according to the backcasted list, and Mexico and Pakistan exiting FCS status. Since Mexico and Pakistan have large populations but relatively low poverty rates, their exit from the list pulls the average poverty rate of FCS up. Conversely, the decline from around 2005 to 2012 is largely explained by Nigeria exiting FCS status and Mexico and Pakistan entering FCS status around this time.

FIGURE 1.6 **Poverty Trends in Economies in FCS and Other Economies, 2000–30**

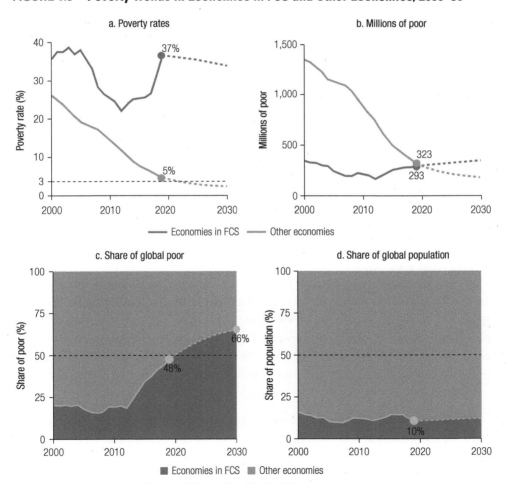

Sources: PovcalNet; UNHCR 2019; IDMC 2019; IMF 2019; United Nations 2019.

Note: Three-year moving averages are used between 2001 and 2018 to smooth out trends. All displaced populations are included in the figures for "Economies in FCS." FCS = fragile and conflict-affected situations.

As the poverty rate in FCS has increased, the number of poor people in economies in FCS has risen from 180 million to nearly 300 million—nearing the number of poor in economies not in FCS (figure 1.6b). Poor people in FCS accounted for 48 percent of all global poor in 2019 (figure 1.6c), even though the share of the global population residing in economies in FCS is just 10 percent (figure 1.6d). If this trend continues, by the end of 2020, the majority of the world's poor will be living in states or economies in FCS.[6]

One can take the analysis one step further and investigate how these patterns will evolve toward 2030. Such an analysis would carry considerable uncertainty. Not only does one need to plausibly estimate the populations of all economies and how their poverty rates will evolve going forward, but assumptions also need to be made about which economies will be in FCS and the size of the displaced population in each economy. Projecting poverty rates in economies in FCS is particularly difficult. Forecasts in GDP per capita generally assume that economies in conflict will recover, as evident in the decreasing poverty rates among economies in FCS projected from 2020 onward (figure 1.6a). In all likelihood, some economies in FCS will be plunged further into conflict, while other economies currently not in FCS will erupt into conflict. Either of these patterns could further exacerbate negative poverty trends in economies in FCS toward 2030. Conversely, if some economies successfully escape conflict, the pattern could improve.

With these caveats in mind, if current trends continue, the share of the world's poor living in economies in FCS could constitute two-thirds of the world's poor by 2030. This is particularly striking given that the share of people living in FCS—under these scenarios—will remain about 10 percent going forward. This again underscores the urgent need to address fragility, conflict, and violence if the global community is to end extreme poverty by 2030.

Economies Chronically in FCS Are Driving the Patterns

The backcasted list of economies in FCS can be used to divide economies into different groups according to how often and when they would have been classified as FCS in the past, using the recent World Bank criteria. In particular, one can distinguish economies chronically in FCS, economies that entered FCS, economies that escaped FCS, economies that move in and out of FCS status, and economies that are hardly ever or never in FCS (table 1.1).

These groups can be used to explore what types of economies are driving the divergent poverty patterns described above. Throughout the period, the highest poverty rates are seen in economies chronically in FCS (figure 1.7a). These economies have poverty rates above 40 percent, with no improvements over the past 10 years. Economies that escaped FCS over the 20-year period used to have poverty rates similar to the chronic FCS, 44 percent in the year 2000. However, over the past two decades, these recovering economies post-FCS have managed to cut their poverty rates by more than half, to 19 percent in 2019. The second-highest poverty rates today are seen among economies that entered FCS over the past 20 years and have remained on the FCS list subsequently. These economies had a poverty rate of about 17 percent 10 years ago but have since seen their poverty rates increase to 23 percent.

In terms of share of poor, the economies chronically in FCS accounted for only 5 percent of the world's poor in 2000 but are projected to contain about a quarter of the world's poor by 2030 (figure 1.7b). Economies in a recurrent pattern of FCS, home to more than one-third of all people living in poverty globally, are likely to account for the largest share of the world's poor by 2030. This underscores the importance of finding solutions both for economies locked in unremitting conflict and those in a cycle of briefly escaping FCS only to plunge back into them.

TABLE 1.1 Backcasted Groups, 2000–19

Group	Definition
Chronic FCS	Economies that would have been classified as FCS every year from 2000 to 2019
Entered FCS	Economies that entered FCS during this period and remained there
Recurrent FCS	Economies that appear on the backcasted list more than twice and move in and out at least twice
Escaped FCS	Economies that appeared on the backcasted list consistently early in the period but since then have fully escaped
Rarely FCS	Economies that appear on the backcasted list at most twice
Never FCS	Economies that never appear on the backcasted list

FIGURE 1.7 Poverty Trends by Backcasted FCS Category

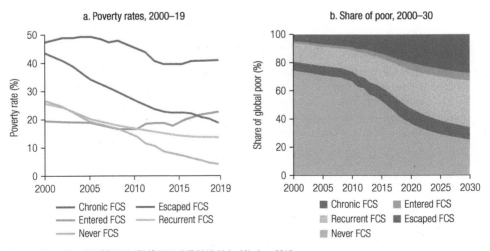

Sources: PovcalNet; UNHCR 2019; IDMC 2019; IMF 2019; United Nations 2019.

Note: See table 1.1 for details on how the categories are defined. Economies that are classified as FCS no more than twice from 2000 to 2019 are included in the "Never FCS" group. FCS = fragile and conflict-affected situations.

Conclusions

As unprecedented numbers of people worldwide have risen from poverty in the past two decades, many countries affected by fragility and conflict are headed in the opposite direction: deeper into the shadows of deprivation and avoidable human suffering. In contrast to global trends, poverty rates in FCS have risen, while the number of people worldwide exposed to conflict has also surged. The number of people living in poverty in FCS will soon exceed the number of poor in all other settings.

As countries in FCS work to improve living standards among their people, income levels are a decisive lever of action and marker of success. In introducing the relationship between FCS and poverty, this chapter has considered poverty primarily in monetary terms. Yet poor people, and especially those living in FCS, face numerous welfare deficits that extend beyond the lack of adequate income or consumption. The task of the next chapter is to analyze these compound challenges and their implications for action against poverty in FCS.

Notes

1. Extreme poverty is measured using the international poverty line of $1.90 per day in 2011 purchasing power parity dollars. Individuals are considered extremely poor if the value of their daily consumption or income falls short of this threshold. See Ferreira et al. (2016) for more information about the derivation of the international poverty line. Any reference to poverty or extreme poverty in this book is based on this definition.

2. Unless otherwise stated, references in this book to economies in FCS are based on the Harmonized List of Fragile Situations produced by the Fragility, Conflict, and Violence Group of the World Bank. See https://www.worldbank.org/en/topic/fragilityconflictviolence/brief/harmonized-list-of-fragile-situations.

   One limitation of using these harmonized lists is that people living in areas of subnational conflict in an otherwise stable economy are not counted when the local conflict is not large enough to place the entire economy on the list. This may lead to a systematic underestimation of the number of people in the world whose lives are affected by conflict.

3. Aside from the institutional and safety reasons for data deprivations in FCS, the financial cost of fielding a survey also matters. Poor economies are generally more data deprived, which could reflect competing demands on scarce resources (Dang, Jolliffe, and Carletto 2019).

4. Displaced people who do not live in camps, but rather relocate to housing structures of some kind, frequently with relatives, are often picked up by household surveys.

5. This number is calculated with reference to the year 2015. The number includes seven economies that were no longer in FCS in 2015 but previously had been, and that had no data since escaping FCS, as indicated in figure 1.3. The number excludes missing data on displaced populations to avoid double counting displaced individuals in economies considered data deprived.

6. Considerable uncertainty surrounds exactly when this will occur. This is not only because the group of economies in FCS will likely change in the years ahead but also because new poverty rates for critical economies, such as Nigeria, are expected in the coming year. If the poverty rate in Nigeria were to be much lower than the most recent estimate, then the exact time when the share of poor in FCS will exceed 50 percent could be delayed.

References

Beegle, Kathleen, and Luc Christiaensen. 2019. *Accelerating Poverty Reduction in Africa.* Washington, DC: World Bank.

Bruederle, Anna, and Roland Hodler. 2018. "Nighttime Lights as a Proxy for Human Development at the Local Level." *PLoS One* 13 (9): https://doi.org/10.1371/journal.pone.0202231.

Dang, H. A., D. Jolliffe, and C. Carletto. 2019. "Data Gaps, Data Incomparability, and Data Imputation: A Review of Poverty Measurement Methods for Data-Scarce Environments." *Journal of Economic Surveys* 33 (3): 757–97.

Ferreira, Francisco H. G., Shaohua Chen, Andrew Dabalen, Yuri Dikhanov, Nada Hamadeh, Dean Jolliffe, Ambar Narayan, Espen Beer Prydz, Ana Revenga, Prem Sangraula, Umar Serajuddin, and Nobuo Yoshida. 2016. "A Global Count of the Extreme Poor in 2012: Data Issues, Methodology and Initial Results." *Journal of Economic Inequality* 14 (2): 141–72.

Henderson, J., Adam Storeygard Vernon, and David N. Weil. 2012. "Measuring economic growth from outer space." *American Economic Review* 102 (2): 994–1028.

Himelein, Kristen, Stephanie Eckman, Siobhan Murray, and Johannes Bauer. 2017. "Alternatives to Full Listing for Second Stage Sampling: Methods and Implications." *Statistical Journal of the IAOS* 33 (3): 701–718.

IDMC (International Displacement Monitoring Centre). 2019. Global International Displacement Database (accessed October 15, 2019), http://www.internal-displacement.org/database/displacement-data.

IMF (International Monetary Fund). 2019. World Economic Outlook Database, October 2019 Edition (accessed October 15, 2019). https://www.imf.org/external/pubs/ft/weo/2019/02/weodata/index.aspx

Jolliffe, D., P. Lanjouw, S. Chen, A. Kraay, C. Meyer, M. Negre, et al. 2014. *A Measured Approach to Ending Poverty and Boosting Shared Prosperity: Concepts, Data, and the Twin Goals.* Washington, DC: World Bank.

LandScan. 2012. High-Resolution Global Population Data Set. Oak Ridge National Laboratory, Oak Ridge, TN (accessed October 15, 2019). https://landscan.ornl.gov.

Pape, Utz Johann, and Johan A. Mistiaen. 2018. "Household Expenditure and Poverty Measures in 60 Minutes: A New Approach with Results from Mogadishu." Policy Research Working Paper 8430, World Bank, Washington, DC.

Pape, Utz Johann, and Philip Randolph Wollburg. 2019. "Estimation of Poverty in Somalia Using Innovative Methodologies." Policy Research Working Paper 8735, World Bank, Washington, DC.

Pinkovskiy, Maxim, and Xavier Sala-i-Martin. 2016. "Lights, Camera . . . Income! Illuminating the National Accounts-Household Surveys Debate." *Quarterly Journal of Economics* 131 (2): 579–631.

Prydz, Espen Beer, Dean Mitchell Jolliffe, Christoph Lakner, Daniel Gerszon Mahler, and Prem Sangraula. 2019. "National Accounts Data Used in Global Poverty Measurement." Global Poverty Monitoring Technical Note 8. Washington, DC: World Bank Group.

PovcalNet. Online analysis data tool. Washington, DC. World Bank. http://iresearch.worldbank.org/PovcalNet/povOnDemand.aspx.

UCDP (Uppsala Conflict Data Program). 2019. *UCDP Conflict Encyclopedia* (accessed October 15, 2019). Sweden: Department of Peace and Conflict Research, Uppsala University. www.ucdp.uu.se.

UNHCR (United Nations High Commissioner for Refugees). 2019. Population Statistics Database (accessed October 15, 2019). http://popstats.unhcr.org/.

United Nations. 2019. *World Population Prospects 2019*. New York: UN Department of Economic and Social Affairs, Population Division. https://population.un.org/wpp/.

World Bank. Harmonized List of Fragile Situations, updated July 1, 2018. Washington, DC: World Bank. https://www.worldbank.org/en/topic/fragilityconflictviolence/brief/harmonized-list-of-fragile -situations.

World Bank. 2018. *Poverty and Shared Prosperity 2018: Piecing Together the Poverty Puzzle.* Washington, DC: World Bank.

World Bank. 2019. *Somali Poverty and Vulnerability Assessment: Findings from Wave 2 of the Somali High Frequency Survey*. Washington, DC: World Bank.

2. Challenges in Multiple Dimensions

Key Messages

- *One in five people in fragile and conflict-affected situations (FCS) suffer from monetary, educational, and infrastructure deprivations simultaneously.*
- *Economies in FCS lag behind non-FCS in all components of human capital.*
- *Conflict deaths and institutional fragility are associated with lower gross domestic product growth rates.*
- *People in economies in FCS are less satisfied with their lives and less hopeful about the future.*

Seeing Beyond Monetary Poverty

The value of an individual's consumption is an important marker of their level of well-being. It signals their ability to obtain food, clothing, shelter, and more. However, some aspects of well-being are not well captured with monetary measures of poverty. One reason for this is that not all goods and services that matter to people are obtained exclusively through markets. Some may be provided for free, or at a lower rate, by governments. This includes infrastructure services, such as clean water and electricity, and other essential components of well-being, such as health and education.

To account for the multiple ways in which poverty manifests itself, while acknowledging the central importance of monetary poverty, the World Bank (2018a) introduced a multidimensional measure of poverty anchored in monetary poverty. This measure of multidimensional poverty classifies individuals as poor if the value of their daily consumption or income falls short of US$1.90, if they are deprived in terms of educational outcomes, and/or if they lack access to the basic services of improved water, improved sanitation, and electricity (more details in box 2.1).

Applying such a multidimensional lens to 87 developing economies, of which 20 are in FCS, reveals that nearly half of all individuals in FCS are multidimensionally poor (figure 2.1).[1] This is in contrast to economies not in FCS, where a much smaller proportion of people, one in five, is multidimensionally poor.

BOX 2.1

The Multidimensional Poverty Measure

The World Bank's Multidimensional Poverty Measure takes inspiration and guidance from the global Multidimensional Poverty Index produced by the United Nations Development Programme in collaboration with the Oxford Poverty and Human Development Initiative. The World Bank's Multidimensional Poverty Measure is composed of three dimensions of well-being with six underlying indicators, as presented in table B2.1.1.

TABLE B2.1.1   Dimensions of Well-Being and Indicators of Deprivation

Dimension	Indicator of deprivation	Weight
Monetary poverty	Daily consumption or income is less than US$1.90 per person	1/3
Education	At least one school-age child up to the age of grade 8 is not enrolled in school	1/6
	No adult in the household (age of grade 9 or above) has completed primary education	1/6
Access to basic infrastructure	The household lacks access to limited-standard drinking water	1/9
	The household lacks access to limited-standard sanitation	1/9
	The household has no access to electricity	1/9

Source: World Bank 2018a.

Note: Limited-standard drinking water is drinking water that comes from an improved source (for example, piped, borehole, protected dug well, rainwater, delivered water). Limited-standard sanitation means using improved sanitation facilities (for example, flush/pour flush to piped sewer system, septic tank, or a composting latrine) (WHO and UNICEF 2017).

Individuals are considered multidimensionally poor if they are deprived in at least one-third of the weighted indicators.

FIGURE 2.1   Monetary and Multidimensional Poverty Are Higher in Economies in FCS

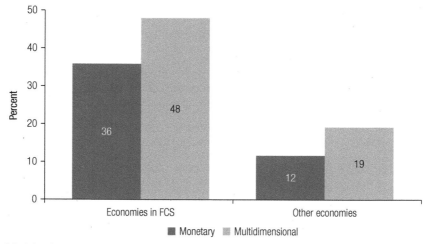

Source: Calculations based on World Bank 2018a.

Note: Excludes high-income economies. FCS = fragile and conflict-affected situations.

Not only are households in FCS more often multidimensionally poor, but poor households in FCS more frequently suffer from multiple deprivations. This makes it harder for them to escape poverty and achieve the lives they want for themselves and their families. For instance, almost a fifth of the population living in FCS experiences deprivations in education, basic infrastructure, and monetary welfare simultaneously, more than three times the rate found in economies not in FCS (figure 2.2). This is particularly the case in economies in FCS in Sub-Saharan Africa. In Burundi, the Democratic Republic of Congo, and Niger, for example, more than a third of the population is estimated to suffer from all three of these forms of deprivation simultaneously. Similarly, 43 percent of individuals in FCS suffer from deprivations in at least two different dimensions of well-being, while the corresponding figure for economies not in FCS is 15 percent.

Yet, once again, data gaps prevent a full picture of the multidimensionality of deprivations in FCS. Whereas just above half of economies in FCS have the data necessary to compute multidimensional poverty, two-thirds of economies not in FCS (excluding high-income economies) have the necessary data.

Although the measure of multidimensional poverty is more encompassing than focusing on monetary poverty alone, important nonmonetary dimensions, such as health outcomes and security outcomes, are still missing due to lack of comparable data across countries. Incorporating such dimensions would likely paint an even

FIGURE 2.2 Overlapping Deprivations Are More Pronounced in Economies in FCS

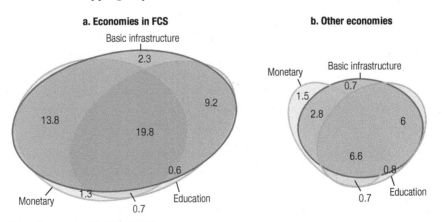

Source: Calculations based on World Bank 2018a.

Note: The diagrams illustrate the types of deprivations that individuals suffer from and the extent to which overlapping deprivations occur. The circle size is proportional to the population share deprived. Summing up all numbers indicates the share of the population that is multidimensionally poor. Summing up all numbers in the orange circle gives the share of the population that is poor in monetary terms, and similarly for the other circles. The number in the center indicates the share of the population that is deprived in all three dimensions simultaneously. The figure excludes high-income economies. FCS = fragile and conflict-affected situations.

more somber picture for economies in FCS, and particularly for women and girls in FCS. For example, the rate of intimate partner violence is 34 percent higher for conflict-affected economies than non-conflict-affected economies (GIWPS and PRIO 2017). This may be because exposure to conflict increases tolerance of domestic violence in adulthood (La Mattina and Shemyakina 2017; Slegh, Barker, and Levtov 2014).

At the indicator level, economies in FCS are also more likely to be without data. For example, 89 percent of economies in FCS have no data since 2015 on the share of people using safely managed drinking water services, while only half of developing economies not in FCS lack this data. Seventy-six percent of economies in FCS have no data since 2015 on the share of people using safely managed sanitation services, while the same number for developing economies not in FCS is 66 percent. Thirty-eight percent of economies in FCS lack data on the share of the population undernourished, while this information is absent in only 9 percent of developing economies not in FCS.[2] Altogether, these data deprivations make it difficult to paint a full picture of the extent of welfare deprivations in FCS, the causes of the deprivations, and policies to address them.

Losing Human Capital—Where It Is Needed Most

Multidimensional deprivation has a trapping effect on individuals and households, in substantial part through impacts on human capital—people's health, education, and skills. Lack of human capital pulls people further from the "productivity frontier"—the ideal full use of their productive capacities.

Economies in FCS generally perform poorly on the World Bank's Human Capital Index (HCI), a measure of how well countries are protecting and developing their human capital (box 2.2). In fact, economies in FCS lag behind non-FCS economies on all six of the indicators that make up the HCI (figure 2.3). Thus, vast unused human potential characterizes families, communities, and economies in FCS. Only a handful of economies in FCS have human capital levels on par with the typical developing economy. Economies in FCS are particularly lagging in the probability of children surviving to age 5 and in learning-adjusted years of school.

The poor performance of economies in FCS becomes even more salient when zooming in on economies in high-intensity conflict, defined as having at least 10 conflict deaths per 100,000 people, and at least 150 in total (or 250, depending on the data source, see appendix C for details). Although only three economies in high-intensity conflict have data on the HCI (Afghanistan, South Sudan, and the Republic of Yemen), these economies suggest that the more severe the conflict, the greater is the distance to the productivity frontier. On average, these three economies lag behind the other FCS economies on all aspects of human capital (figure 2.3).

The Human Capital Index

The Human Capital Index (HCI) calculates the contributions of health and education to worker productivity (Kraay 2018). The index score ranges from zero to one, and measures the productivity as a future worker of a child born today, relative to the benchmark of full health and complete education. It has six components:

1. **Probability of Survival to Age 5,** calculated by subtracting the under-5 mortality rate from 1
2. **Fraction of Children Under 5 Not Stunted,** calculated by subtracting stunting rates from 1
3. **Adult Survival Rate,** calculated by subtracting the mortality rate for 15–60-year-olds from 1
4. **Expected Years of School,** calculated as the sum of age-specific enrollment rates between ages 4 and 17 (Age-specific enrollment rates are approximated using school enrollment rates at different levels.)
5. **Harmonized Test Scores,** utilizing a database of harmonized scores across major international student-achievement testing programs measured in TIMSS-equivalent units, where 300 is minimal attainment and 625 is advanced attainment
6. **Learning-Adjusted Years of School,** calculated by multiplying the estimates of expected years of school by the ratio of most recent harmonized test scores to 625, where 625 corresponds to advanced attainment on the TIMSS

Note: TIMSS, the Trends in International Mathematics and Science Study, is conducted by the International Association for the Evaluation of Educational Achievement. See: https://www.iea.nl/studies/iea/timss.

FIGURE 2.3   Economies in FCS Are Lagging in All Aspects of Human Capital

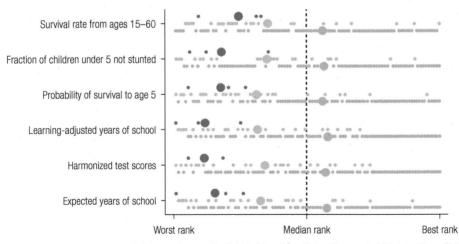

Source: World Bank 2018b.

Note: The figure excludes high-income countries. Economies in high-intensity conflict are defined as having at least 10 conflict deaths per 100,000 population according to the Armed Conflict Location and Event Data Project (ACLED) and Uppsala Conflict Data Program (UCDP), along with at least 150 total conflict deaths according to UCDP or at least 250 according to ACLED. See appendix C for details. FCS = fragile and conflict-affected situations.

FCS and Growth: Negative Associations

When people cannot secure the health and skills they need to be fully productive, the waste of potential compromises not only individual earnings and life trajectories but also countries' future growth. This risks trapping economies in fragility and poverty, since one fundamental way that countries can lift people out of poverty is through economic growth whose benefits are equitably distributed. Economies suffering from institutional fragility or conflict generally have lower growth rates than economies not in fragility and conflict (Blattman and Miguel 2010; Rodrik 1999).

Economies that in a given year experienced fewer than 100 conflict deaths per 100,000 had on average real per capita growth rates around 2 percent that year. This rate declines rapidly for economies that experienced more conflict deaths and becomes negative for economies that have experienced more than 1,000 conflict deaths per 100,000 (figure 2.4a). This finding is not too different from results reported by Mueller (2016), who used geolocalized data for Africa to show that experiencing more than 50 conflict fatalities reduced growth by about 4.4 percentage points. Likewise, economies exhibiting institutional fragility as measured by low Country Policy and Institutional Assessment (CPIA) scores have experienced lower growth rates (figure 2.4b).[3]

The negative correlation between conflict and growth means fewer economic opportunities for the poor in FCS in the short term. Slow growth today also affects the future. A weak economy makes it more difficult for countries to generate resources for the long-term investments in human capital that are needed to break cycles of deprivation.

FIGURE 2.4 **Growth Is Negatively Correlated with Conflict Deaths and Fragility**

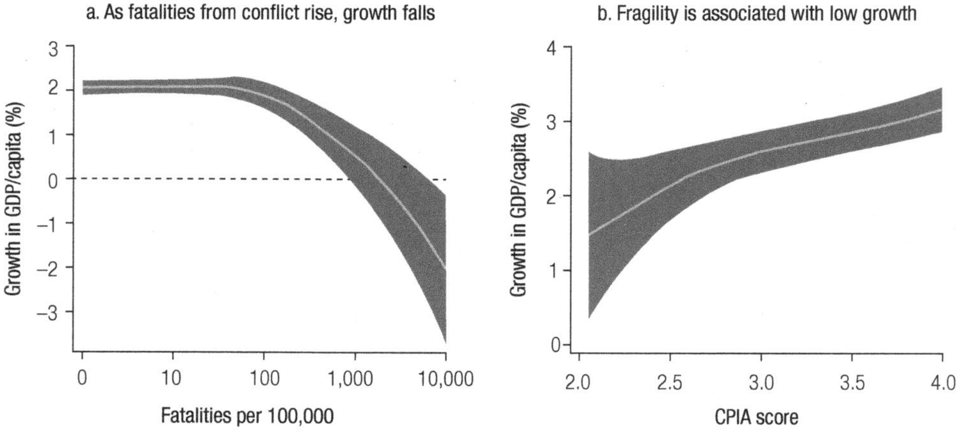

Sources: UCDP 2019; ACLED 2019; World Development Indicators (https://data.worldbank.org/indicator/NY.GDP.PCAP.PP.KD)
Note: Fatalities are top-coded at 10,000 per 100,000. The figure uses ACLED data for fatalities and supplements with UCDP for cases with no ACLED data. CPIA = Country Policy and Institutional Assessment; UCDP = Uppsala Conflict Data Program.

Picturing a Better Future?

The analysis so far has shown that people in economies in FCS are doing worse on a range of objective indicators important for their standard of living. Another question pertains to how individuals living amid conflict, violence, and fragility *perceive* their own situation. Do they feel that life is going well? Do they have positive hopes for the future? Perceptions about life are important in their own right in supporting people's mental well-being, but poor self-assessments and low aspirations also matter instrumentally, as they can lead to a sense of hopelessness materializing in less productive lives, and ultimately to further unrest (Swee, Zhan, and Powdthavee 2019). In the context of education, parents having higher educational aspirations for their children has been shown to increase enrollment, time spent in school, and schooling expenditures (Bernard et al. 2019).

Living in fragility, conflict, or violence is associated with lower satisfaction with life (figure 2.5a). When asked to rank their life quality along a spectrum from the worst to the best possible, more than 50 percent of all individuals in a typical economy in FCS think that their life is closer to the worst possible than to the best possible, while the corresponding figure for economies not in FCS is 37 percent. Whereas 9 percent of individuals in a typical economy in FCS think that their life is the worst possible life,

FIGURE 2.5 People Living in FCS Are Less Satisfied with Their Life and Community

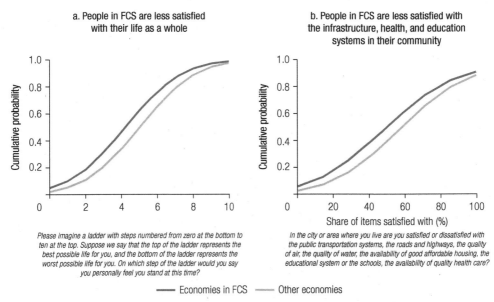

a. People in FCS are less satisfied with their life as a whole

b. People in FCS are less satisfied with the infrastructure, health, and education systems in their community

Please imagine a ladder with steps numbered from zero at the bottom to ten at the top. Suppose we say that the top of the ladder represents the best possible life for you, and the bottom of the ladder represents the worst possible life for you. On which step of the ladder would you say you personally feel you stand at this time?

In the city or area where you live are you satisfied or dissatisfied with the public transportation systems, the roads and highways, the quality of air, the quality of water, the availability of good affordable housing, the educational system or the schools, the availability of quality health care?

—— Economies in FCS —— Other economies

Source: Gallup World Poll 2016.

Note: The figures compare attitudes in a typical economy in FCS with a typical economy not in FCS. The figures use the economies classified as FCS in 2016 to be consistent with the timing of the Gallup data. This includes Afghanistan, Central African Republic, Chad, Congo, Dem. Rep., Côte d'Ivoire, Haiti, Iraq, Kosovo, Lebanon, Liberia, Libya, Madagascar, Mali, Myanmar, Sierra Leone, Somalia, South Sudan, Togo, West Bank and Gaza, Yemen, Rep., and Zimbabwe. Other economies were classified as in FCS but lack Gallup data. FCS = fragile and conflict-affected situations.

the corresponding proportion in a typical non-FCS economy is just 5 percent, lower by almost half.

Individuals in FCS are not only less satisfied with their own life, they are also less satisfied with many features of the communities in which they live. In a typical economy in FCS, 53 percent of individuals are more dissatisfied than satisfied with their community's public transportation system, roads and highways, quality of air, quality of water, affordable housing, educational system, and health care (figure 2.5b). In a typical economy not in FCS, this number falls to 41 percent.

One could imagine that, due to the hardship people in FCS have faced, their future quality of life can only go in one direction—upward. Yet a troubling finding is that people in FCS express little hope for positive change. Only half of individuals in a typical FCS economy think that their standard of living is getter better rather than worse (figure 2.6a). This is lower than in developing economies not in FCS across all regions. In East Asia and Pacific, for example, nearly three in four people living in non-FCS believe that life is getting better. People in economies in FCS are also less likely to believe that children in their communities have the opportunity to grow and learn. Only 54 percent of individuals in the typical economy in FCS believe this is the case, while the figure is at least 62 percent in non-FCS across all regions, and as high as 86 percent in East Asia and Pacific (figure 2.6b).

FIGURE 2.6   Most People Living in FCS Also Doubt that Things Will Get Better

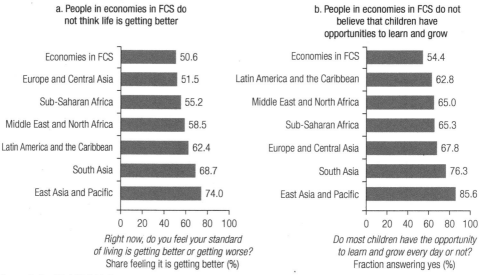

Source: Gallup World Poll 2016.

Note: The figures compare attitudes in a typical economy in FCS with a typical economy not in FCS. The figures use the economies classified as FCS in 2016 to be consistent with the timing of the Gallup data. Only developing economies are included, and economies in FCS are excluded from the regional averages. Economies in FCS for this analysis include: Afghanistan, Central African Republic, Chad, Congo, Dem. Rep., Côte d'Ivoire, Haiti, Iraq, Kosovo, Lebanon, Liberia Libya, Madagascar, Mali, Myanmar, Sierra Leone, Somalia, South Sudan, Togo, West Bank and Gaza, Yemen, Rep., and Zimbabwe. Other economies were classified as in FCS but lack Gallup data. FCS = fragile and conflict-affected situations.

Conclusions

Data confirm that the poor in FCS are more likely than poor people elsewhere to suffer multiple forms of deprivation simultaneously. Common dimensions of deprivation and distress in FCS include: acute violence or posttraumatic experiences; lack of basic infrastructure (for example, water and electricity); and no access to quality health care or education. These factors erode multiple dimensions of poor people's human capital. For countries, lost human capital means lost economic growth.

A critical question for countries in FCS is, how long will these effects last? While a territory is in active armed conflict, reducing poverty is probably not a realistic aim. But once the fighting stops, many of the acute causes of multidimensional deprivation may subside, enabling countries to get back on the path of economic progress and poverty reduction. Anecdotally, recent history offers notable examples of countries that have shown remarkable economic resilience following conflict—although counterexamples also abound.

This question has policy implications. Policy responses and investment decisions will be very different, if there is a reasonable probability that conflict's poverty and welfare impacts will prove short-lived once active fighting ends. The following chapter will shed light on this issue through an analysis based on human capital.

Notes

1. The number of economies for which multidimensional poverty can be calculated is less than the number of economies for which monetary poverty can be calculated, since the former, in addition to monetary poverty, requires data on educational attainment and access to basic infrastructure. Not all household surveys capture this information.

2. All of these values are calculated through the World Bank's World Development Indicators, based on the information available as of November 18, 2019.

3. Needless to say, the figures cited do not demonstrate causal relationships among conflict, fragility, and growth and show only that they are negatively associated. Studying possible causal relations among these phenomena is complicated by a hoax of endogeneity issue (Ray and Esteban 2017). In addition, growth in FCS is more likely to reflect the fact that economies in FCS start from a low base, and that growth is often driven by unsustainable foreign aid receipts. The association between lack of growth and conflict would likely be stronger when accounting for these two factors.

References

ACLED (Armed Conflict Location and Event Data Project). 2019. Political violence and protest database (accessed October 15, 2019). https://www.acleddata.com.

Bernard, Tanguy, Stefan Dercon, Kate Orkin, and Alemayehu Seyoum Taffesse. 2019. "Parental Aspirations for Children's Education: Is There a 'Girl Effect'? Experimental Evidence from Rural Ethiopia." *AEA Papers and Proceedings, American Economic Association* 109 (May): 27–132.

Blattman, Christopher, and Edward Miguel. 2010. "Civil War." *Journal of Economic Literature* 48 (1): 3–57.

Gallup. 2016. *World Poll 2016*. Database (accessed October 15, 2019). https://www.gallup
.com/analytics/232838/world-poll.aspx.

GIWPS and PRIO (Georgetown Institute for Women, Peace and Security and Peace Research Institute
Oslo). 2017. *Women, Peace and Security Index 2017/18: Tracking Sustainable Peace through
Inclusion, Justice, and Security for Women*. Washington, DC: GIWPS and PRIO.

Kraay, Aart C. 2018. "Methodology for a World Bank Human Capital Index." Policy Research Working
Paper 8593, World Bank, Washington, DC.

La Mattina, Giulia, and Olga N. Shemyakina. 2017. "Domestic Violence and Childhood Exposure to
Armed Conflict: Attitudes and Experiences." Working paper 255, Households in Conflict
Network, University of Sussex, Brighton. http://www.hicn.org/wordpress/wp-content
/uploads/2012/06/HiCN-WP255.pdf.

Mueller, Hannes. 2016. "Growth and Violence: Argument for a per Capita Measure of Civil War."
Economica 83 (331): 473–9.

Ray, Debraj, and Joan Esteban. 2017. "Conflict and Development." *Annual Review of
Economics* 9: 263–93.

Rodrik, Dani. 1999. "Where Did All the Growth Go? External Shocks, Social Conflict, and Growth
Collapses." *Journal of Economic Growth* 4 (4): 385–412.

Slegh, H., G. Barker, and R. Levtov. 2014. *Gender Relations, Sexual and Gender-Based Violence and the
Effects of Conflict on Women and Men in North Kivu, Eastern Democratic Republic of Congo:
Results from the International Men and Gender Equality Survey (IMAGES)*. Washington, DC, and
Cape Town, South Africa: Promundo-US and Sonke Gender Justice.

Swee, Eik, Haikun Zhan, and Nattavudh Powdthavee. 2019. "Do Perceptions of Economic Well-Being
Predict the Onset of War and Peace?" Working paper 12650, Institute of Labor Economics,
Bonn.

UCDP (Uppsala Conflict Data Program). 2019. UCDP Conflict Encyclopedia (database), Department
of Peace and Conflict Research, Uppsala University, Uppsala, Sweden (accessed October 15,
2019). www.ucdp.uu.se.

WHO and UNICEF (World Health Organization and United Nations Children's Fund). 2017. *Progress
on Drinking Water, Sanitation and Hygiene: 2017 Update and SDG Baselines*. Geneva: WHO.

World Bank. 2018a. *Poverty and Shared Prosperity 2018: Piecing Together the Poverty Puzzle*.
Washington, DC: World Bank.

World Bank. 2018b. "The Human Capital Project." World Bank, Washington, DC. https://www
.worldbank.org/en/publication/human-capital.

3. Long-Term Effects of Conflict on Poverty and Welfare

Key Messages

- *Exposure to conflict in childhood leads to poorer lifetime health.*
- *Conflict's negative health effects extend intergenerationally; the original victims' children also have worse outcomes.*
- *Evidence generally shows negative effects of conflict on educational outcomes; issues such as gendered impacts need more research.*
- *Human capital losses due to conflict lower people's lifetime productivity and earnings and reduce intergenerational socioeconomic mobility.*

Introduction

The immediate effects of conflict are starkly clear. They include deaths and injuries, population displacement, the destruction of assets, and the disruption of social and economic systems. But one day the fighting stops, and life in conflict-affected areas gradually returns to normal. Or does it? How long do the economic and welfare effects of armed conflict typically persist? In particular, how long will these effects constrain growth and limit countries' ability to reduce poverty? To set strategy for the global poverty endgame, this is a crucial question.

This chapter summarizes current evidence on the long-term welfare impacts of conflict and fragility. The analysis focuses on key dimensions of human capital—health and education. A human capital lens reveals that substantial negative impacts of fragile and conflict-affected situations (FCS) can extend across decades and even generations. After the guns fall silent, conflict leaves a legacy of damaged human capital that will lower productivity, weaken growth, and slow poverty reduction far into the future.

Conflict through a Human Capital Lens

To assess conflict's long-term economic and welfare effects, what methods are most helpful? One line of recent research has focused on tracing broad economic indicators through periods of conflict and recovery.[1] Taken as a whole, this literature yields no consensus on whether countries fully recover economic activity after conflict and, if they do, how long the process takes.[2]

A different way to evaluate the long-term impacts of conflict on welfare and economic development is to focus on human capital—people's health, education, and skills—increasingly recognized as a critical determinant of countries' economic performance (World Bank 2018). Barro and Sala-i-Martin (2004) argued that the recovery of growth after conflict likely depends on whether and how quickly human capital adjusts, as it is typically slower to rebuild than physical capital. An extensive body of research has since emerged on conflict's human capital effects.

The human capital focus is critical for welfare and poverty reduction, not least because health and education have been shown to determine long-term living standards for individuals and households (for example, Strauss and Thomas 1998). The remainder of this chapter summarizes evidence on the impact of conflict on health and education. Recent studies confirm both short-term impacts and substantial longer-term compromise to human capital in postconflict settings.

The Impact of Conflict on Human Capital: Health

Children and young people embody a society's future. By harming children, war puts that future directly at risk. Accordingly, many studies of conflict and human capital have focused on children's health. Such studies consistently show that, in addition to the physical wounds inflicted by armed violence, conflict harms children's health in less visible ways that also carry consequences for long-term welfare. Importantly, children's health can be affected both directly and through effects on their caregivers, particularly their mothers (Kadir, Shenoda, and Goldhagen 2019; Wagner et al. 2018).

The literature establishes a firm causal link between violent conflict and a range of negative health outcomes among children. Given the limited availability of long-term panel data in conflict settings, most evidence is available on outcomes that can be measured in the short and medium terms but that may proxy long-term health and well-being. These include children's height-for-age. For example, Minoiu and Shemyakina (2014) studied the impact of the 2002–07 civil conflict in Côte d'Ivoire on children's stature. They found that the conflict reduced height-for-age z-scores of children exposed to the war and that this negative impact increased with the time children were exposed to the conflict. Other studies have reported similar patterns for a wide variety of FCS.[3] Evidence that conflict negatively impacts children's stature takes on added importance in light of the well-documented correlation between height and earnings. In both high- and low-income settings, taller people make more money, on average (Bossavie et al. 2017; Case and Paxson 2008; Schultz 2003). Thus, by compromising children's healthy development as proxied by height, conflict exposure puts individuals at a lifelong economic disadvantage.

Health Damage across Generations

Not only do children's conflict-related health losses often persist into their adult life, but new studies show that conflict's health impacts extend intergenerationally.

In particular, two recent studies on the long-term effects of conflict on health provide evidence for intergenerational transmission of adverse human capital effects. Akresh et al. (2018) assess the impact of the 1967–70 Nigerian Civil War on health and education among people (mostly women) exposed to the conflict in their growth years and on their children born later. The researchers find that exposure to the conflict had negative human capital impacts on the populations directly exposed, including reduced stature in adulthood, increased likelihood of being overweight, and lower educational attainment for women. The study also shows that the children of women (not men) exposed to the war in their adolescence have lower human capital as a result of the conflict. They have higher neonatal, infant, and child mortality rates than children of women not exposed to the war, are more likely to be stunted (14 percentage points), and are more likely to be underweight (22 percentage points) if they survive.

In Nepal, Phadera (2019) studies the impact of childhood exposure to the 1996–2006 civil conflict on women's stature and on their children's height and weight. He establishes a robust causal impact of conflict exposure in childhood, in particular, exposure starting very early in the growth period, on women's final adult height. Moreover, he provides further evidence for second-generation effects on the health of children whose mothers were exposed to conflict: these children have lower weight-for-height, weight-for-age, and body mass index z-scores (box 3.1).

Conflict, Mental Health, and Income

The current literature provides more limited but suggestive evidence on other longer-term health outcomes that may be affected by conflict: notably mental health. For example, Singhal (forthcoming) uses the Miguel and Roland (2011) data on US bombing campaigns in Vietnam to assess the impact of early life war exposure on mental health in adulthood. He finds that adults who were exposed to the war during childhood report greater depressive symptoms up to 30 years after the conflict.

Some studies trace an explicit link from conflict through mental health to lost income. Bratti, Mendolab, and Mirandac (2016) study the impact of the 1992–95 Bosnia and Herzegovina conflict on mental health and individual labor market outcomes six

Unfortunate Mothers and Unfortunate Children: Intergenerational Health Impacts of Civil Conflict in Nepal

Nepal's 10-year civil war

In 1996 the Communist Party of Nepal Maoist launched an armed struggle against the Nepali state. This insurgency developed into an entrenched and often brutal countrywide civil war over the following decade, resulting in more than 13,000 fatalities; considerable infrastructure destruction; interruptions in the delivery of basic services, notably health care; and pervasive feelings of fear, insecurity, and mental stress among Nepali citizens. In addition to the direct physical and mental trauma inflicted on people, the conflict reduced economic activity and resulted in widespread income and nutritional shocks. A new study (Phadera 2019) looks at the impact of childhood exposure to Nepal's civil conflict on women's adult health 10 years after the end of the conflict, as well as on their children's health outcomes, that is, intergenerational transmission.

Health and economic damage in the first generation

The study finds that exposure to conflict starting in infancy had a highly significant and negative impact on attained adult height. Each additional month of exposure decreased a women's adult height by 1.36 millimeters. These results are especially important, given increasing evidence of the lasting impacts of stunting and slow height growth early in life on overall physical and cognitive development, school achievement, economic productivity, and maternal reproductive outcomes. Thus, the Nepal findings imply that many women exposed to the civil conflict as children have suffered not only worse health, but lower lifetime labor productivity and incomes.

Harms extend to the second generation

The negative health impacts of conflict extend beyond those persons directly exposed to the violence. The second generation continues to register negative impacts, as well. The study finds that a mother's exposure to conflict in her childhood is detrimental to her own children's health. Children born to an exposed woman have lower weight-for-height and body mass index z-scores. What could explain such effects? The study shows that women exposed to the conflict during childhood have more children and live in poorer households as adults. The authors suggest that the combination of these two factors may decrease parents' ability to invest in their children's human capital during the critical period of physical development. This second-generation human capital shortfall is again likely to translate into reduced individual productivity and earnings, ultimately weighing on economic growth.

years after the conflict. Theirs is one of few currently available papers that incorporate outcomes used to measure economic welfare. They find that self-reported war trauma increased the likelihood of suffering from depression and led to large reductions in the probability of labor force participation (28.3 percentage points or 78 percent), in weekly working hours (12.2 hours less per week), and in labor income (57 percent).[4]

The Impact of Conflict on Human Capital: Education

The impact of violent conflict on educational outcomes has also received substantial attention in the literature. On balance, evidence across diverse contexts suggests that conflict does have a negative impact on educational attainment.[5] However, differing results have been reported for different gender and age groups, and some questions around short- versus long-term effects demand further research.

Several studies have found lower educational achievement and reduced lifetime earnings in the wake of conflict. Examining the Zimbabwean civil war that ended in the early 1980s, Alderman, Hoddinott, and Kinsey (2006) find that the conflict had a negative impact on the number of grades completed in adolescence through a reduction in height-for-age z-scores during childhood, a proxy for malnutrition. The authors use established values for the returns to education in the Zimbabwean manufacturing sector to estimate that their findings suggest a reduction in lifetime earnings of 14 percent for people whose educational trajectories were affected by the conflict. Akresh and de Walque (2008) likewise find a strong negative educational effect of Rwanda's 1994 genocide, with school-age children exposed to the genocide losing almost one-half year of completed schooling and being 15 percentage points less likely to complete third or fourth grade six years after the conflict.[6]

While the literature has focused primarily on children who were of school age during the conflicts studied, Bundervoet and Fransen (2018) assess the long-run educational impact of exposure to the Rwandan genocide in utero. By doing so, they shed light on an additional mechanism through which conflict can impact long-term educational outcomes and eventually living standards—the development of cognitive functions (box 3.2).

León (2012), analyzing civil conflict in Peru, likewise finds that conflict exposure in utero reduces educational attainment. In the short term, the Peruvian civil war compromised educational attainment among children who were in utero, in early childhood, or of preschool age, as well as among those who had already started school when exposed to the conflict. In the long run, however, León reports that only shocks in the prebirth/in utero period have lasting effects, while children who experienced shocks in early childhood or preschool age recover partially, and those who had already started school fully catch up to peers who were not exposed to violence.

Mixed Evidence on Gendered Impacts

Does conflict affect educational outcomes differently by gender? Several studies suggest this is the case, but they diverge on whether males or females fare worse. For example, Dabalen and Paul (2014) find that armed conflict in Côte d'Ivoire resulted in a larger

The Educational Impact of Shocks in Utero: Children Exposed to the Rwandan Genocide during Fetal Development Showed Reduced Educational Attainment 18 Years Later

Conflict and cognitive development

The literature on the educational impact of violent conflict has usually focused on exposure at school age. However, Bundervoet and Fransen (2018) study the long-run impact of exposure to the Rwandan genocide in utero on years of schooling, the likelihood of starting primary and secondary school, and the likelihood of completing primary school. Results suggest that conflict-related disruptions of fetal cognitive development may impact children's subsequent educational outcomes and ultimately living standards.

Rwanda's genocide

The Rwandan genocide took place amid civil war and continuous tensions between the country's two main ethnic groups, the Hutu and the Tutsi. On April 6, 1994, extremist Hutu militias, the Rwandan Armed Forces, and police forces mobilized the civilian Hutu population to annihilate the Tutsi minority, as well as moderate Hutus. The genocide took place over three months, ending in July 1994 and resulting in the killing of between 500,000 and 1,000,000 people (7 to 14 percent of Rwanda's total population) and approximately 75 percent of the Tutsi population.

In utero exposure to conflict worsens educational outcomes

The research shows that exposure to the genocide in utero decreased educational attainment by 0.3 years and the likelihood of completing primary school by 8 percent. The impact on years of schooling was stronger for females and for individuals exposed to the genocide in the first trimester of gestation. Moreover, focusing only on exposed children reveals a continuous duration-of-exposure effect. Each additional month of exposure in utero decreased educational attainment by 0.21 years of schooling. The authors do not attempt to quantify the economic impacts of the conflict-related educational shortfalls they report, which they argue may partly reflect children's compromised cognitive development. Such analysis of economic losses represents a task for future research. Cognitive skills are increasingly recognized as a dimension of human capital that shapes individuals' economic outcomes and countries' competitiveness, underlining the importance of fully understanding this pathway.

drop in average years of education for males than females. This finding is echoed by Swee (2015) in the context of Bosnia and Herzegovina. Cohorts there that were most affected by the war were less likely to complete secondary schooling (although not primary schooling), and the effect was much stronger for males than for females and for draftee male cohorts. Singh and Shemyakina (2016), on the contrary, find that the 1981–93 Punjab insurgency negatively affected girls' educational attainment, while there was no effect, or even a positive effect, for boys. In Tajikistan, violent conflict reduced the likelihood of girls' completing mandatory schooling, with no comparable effect observed for boys (Shemyakina 2011).

Do Methods Bias Results?

Two recent studies differ methodologically from most previous research on conflict and education in that they use individual-level panel data.[7] Pivovarova and Swee (2015) focused on the Nepalese civil conflict and found that it did not have an impact on schooling attainment. The authors argue that their individual fixed-effects panel regression specification controls for unobserved heterogeneity at the individual level, while results obtained using conventional difference-in-difference specification suffer from upward bias. However, Bertoni et al. (2019) also use individual-level panel data to study the impact of violent conflict on education, with different results. They focus on the Boko Haram conflict in North-East Nigeria during the period 2009–16 and find a negative short-term effect of conflict on general school enrollment, as well as longer-term reductions in years of education completed among conflict-affected children (box 3.3).

BOX 3.3

Education Is Forbidden: The Boko Haram Conflict Reduced School Enrollment and Educational Attainment in North-East Nigeria

The Boko Haram insurgency

The terrorist group Boko Haram has been fighting against the Nigerian government with the objective of establishing an Islamic state in the country since 2009. Faithful to its name, which can be translated as "(Western) education is forbidden," Boko Haram has targeted the Nigerian education system, mainly assaulting schools, students, and teachers in North-East Nigeria in the states of Adamawa, Bauchi, Borno, Gombe, Taraba, and Yobe. Bertoni et al. (2019) study the impact of the Boko-Haram conflict in North-East Nigeria during the period 2009 to 2016 on school enrollment and educational attainment.

Conflict reduced school enrollment

The study finds that a one standard deviation increase in the number of fatalities within a five-kilometer radius of a child's village reduced school enrollment probability by 3 percentage points. The conflict had a more severe impact on education for children who were no longer of mandatory school age and for whom the opportunity costs of continuing schooling were larger in the event of a conflict. The authors do not find any differential effects by gender, religion, or type of residential location. Moreover, all types of conflict measures yielded a negative and highly significant effect on school enrollment. The effect of conflict events initiated by Boko Haram was, however, smaller in magnitude, suggesting that exposure to insecurity and violence in general reduces school enrollment.

Conflict reduced years of education completed

A one standard deviation increase in the total number of fatalities occurring over the 2009 to 2016 period in a five-kilometer radius of a child's village led to a reduction of 0.6 years of education completed. This is an 11 percent drop in the average educational attainment observed during the period of analysis (5.2 years of education). The negative impact of the conflict on educational attainment is more pronounced for boys, partly because boys had a significantly higher average number of years of education than girls before the conflict. The conflict did not have differential effects by type of residential location, religion, or migration status.

Conflict and Intergenerational Socioeconomic Mobility

In large part through its effects on education, conflict also reduces intergenerational socioeconomic mobility—younger people's likelihood of enjoying better socioeconomic outcomes than their parents and outcomes that are less determined by their parents' rank in society.

The higher the number of conflict deaths to which individuals are exposed before or during their primary school age, the lower the probability they will attain a higher educational level than both their parents (figure 3.1a). Taking educational attainment as a rough proxy for socioeconomic status, this means that individuals' rates of absolute intergenerational mobility decline as the intensity of their childhood conflict exposure rises (Box 3.4 explains how intergenerational mobility is defined and measured.). Individuals exposed to no conflict deaths during their childhood have, on average, more than a 55 percent chance of surpassing both of their parents in education. Individuals exposed to high degrees of violence—10,000 conflict deaths per 100,000 people in the setting of their formative years—have around a 40 percent chance of doing so.

Not only do individuals living in countries with many conflict deaths have a lower probability of doing better than their parents, but their socioeconomic rank is also more likely to be determined by those of their parents. Individuals not living in countries with many conflict deaths by the time they exit primary school are able to

FIGURE 3.1   Economies with Many Conflict Deaths Are Less Intergenerationally Mobile

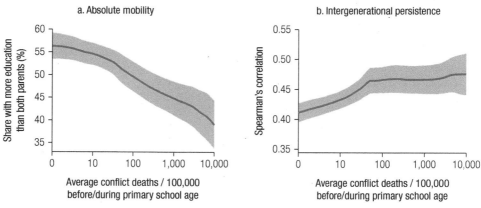

a. Absolute mobility

b. Intergenerational persistence

Source: Global Database on Intergenerational Mobility 2018; UCDP 2019.

Note: The figure uses cohorts born in 1989 or 1990 covering 105 economies and looks at the average conflict deaths per 100,000 inhabitants in each economy during the cohorts' first 12 years of life (converted to a logarithmic scale), that is, from 1989 to 2000 or from 1990 to 2001. The conflict death variable is top-coded at 10,000, which impacts only Rwanda. Intergenerational persistence is measured using Spearman's correlation, which is a measure of statistical dependence between the rankings of two variables, here children's years of schooling and parents' years of schooling. The higher the correlation, the more strongly parents' educational rank predicts their children's educational rank. See box 3.4 for details.

Measures of Intergenerational Mobility

Intergenerational mobility concerns socioeconomic movements between generations. Estimates of intergenerational mobility require data on two generations, which in turn requires panel data or retrospective questions where respondents are asked to comment on the living standards of their parents. Since such data are often unreliable and unavailable in the space of income or consumption, here intergenerational mobility in education is used, utilizing the database in Narayan et al. (2018), which covers 146 economies. Two distinct concepts of intergenerational mobility exist, absolute and relative.

Absolute intergenerational mobility

Absolute intergenerational mobility measures the extent to which the current generation has managed to climb the economic ladder relative to the previous generation. One measure of absolute mobility in education is the share of individuals that have strictly more education than both their parents, where education is measured in five categories: less than primary education, primary, lower secondary, upper secondary, and tertiary. Following this definition, by construction it is impossible to have more education than your parents when one of them has achieved tertiary education. Thus, only individuals whose parents have not obtained tertiary education are considered.

Relative intergenerational mobility

Relative intergenerational mobility is tied to the notion that individuals ought to have equal opportunities in life. In particular, relative intergenerational mobility is the extent to which every individual's position on the economic ladder is independent of the position of the individual's parents. The reverse of relative mobility could be called intergenerational persistence. A measure of intergenerational persistence in education is Spearman's correlation between a cohort's level of education and their parents' level of education. The higher the correlation, the more parents' rank in society predicts their children's rank and the lower the relative mobility. When relative mobility is lower, some children are, on expectation, off to a disadvantaged start even before they are born.

Although the two concepts are related, one may exist without the other (Narayan et al. 2018). If all individuals in a generation climb two rungs relative to their parents without passing or being passed by anyone else in that generation, then there is absolute intergenerational mobility but no relative intergenerational mobility. Conversely, a society may exhibit high relative mobility but not necessarily high absolute intergenerational mobility if all individuals in the current generation are on rungs that are different from the rungs occupied by their parents, while the current generation on average has the same level of education.

obtain outcomes rather independent of their parents, with a correlation between parents' and children's outcomes of around 0.4 (figure 3.1b, see box 3.4 for details on the measure). The educational outcomes of individuals exposed to many conflict deaths are more tied to that of their parents, with a correlation coefficient nearing 0.5. This intergenerational persistence—or lack of relative mobility—signifies that in economies exposed to violence and conflict, individuals face reduced opportunities in life.

These patterns could potentially be explained by a number of reasons other than conflict deaths. It may be that the economies that experienced many conflict deaths also happen to be economies that were already more unequal, spent less on education, or shared other patterns that tend to constrain intergenerational mobility. To understand whether conflict is one of the main drivers of these patterns, it is constructive to look at case studies over time.[8] Intergenerational mobility is well suited for this purpose, since mobility can be estimated for each cohort alive that has completed its educational attainment, allowing for time trends between circa 1940 and 1990.

Iraq and Vietnam provide interesting case studies. In Iraq, the 1980–88 Iran-Iraq war and the ensuing 1990–91 Gulf War implied that cohorts born before about 1969 were able to finish primary school without being affected by conflict, while later cohorts were affected. Vietnam's war with the United States from 1955 to 1975 implied that early cohorts were impacted by war while later cohorts were not.

In Iraq, absolute mobility was on an upward trend for more than two decades before the war with the Islamic Republic of Iran. Among individuals born in 1940, only 25 percent surpassed the educational attainment of both their parents. However, by 1968, the last cohort to reach age 12 and complete primary school before the Iran conflict enjoyed absolute mobility of more than 60 percent. In the following decades, likely due to the multiple wars in which Iraq was involved, this rate declined back to around 35 percent (figure 3.2a). Likewise, intergenerational persistence was low before the wars started, but as soon as they did, it increased rapidly, from around 0.3 in 1968 to 0.5 in 1990 (figure 3.2b). This suggests that the wars reinforced social class divisions and made it harder for the poorest to climb the societal ladder.

Vietnam presents a similar picture. People able to complete primary school before the war with the United States began claiming large death tolls in the 1960s had very high probabilities of surpassing their parents in education, upward of 80 percent. For the decades that followed, this number fell to 65 percent, and after the war ended, Vietnam managed to raise this number back up to 85 percent for the cohort born in 1990 (figure 3.2c). Likewise, intergenerational persistence increased over the duration of the war, from about 0.45 to 0.65. After the war ended, it fell back to 0.5 (figure 3.2d).

These case studies point to conflict and violence exerting negative, large, and lasting impacts on exposed individuals' chances of surpassing their parents' social and economic outcomes.

FIGURE 3.2 Intergenerational Mobility in Iraq and Vietnam over Time

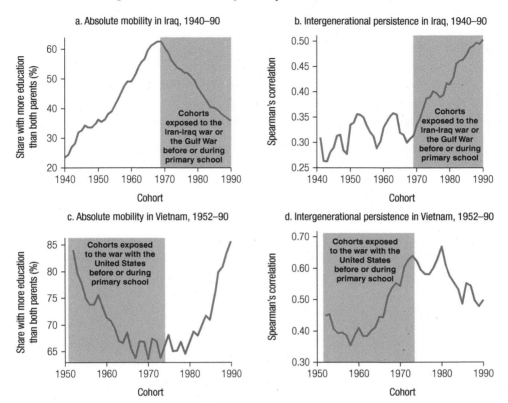

Source: Global Database on Intergenerational Mobility 2018. The Iraq data is based on the 2010 Iraqi Household Socio-Economic Survey, while the Vietnamese data is based on the 2012 STEP Skills Measurement Household Survey, which covers urban areas in Vietnam.

Note: The figure shows absolute mobility and intergenerational persistence for each cohort. Five-year moving averages are used to increase the number of observations. Only cohorts with at least 250 observations are shown. Intergenerational persistence is measured using Spearman's correlation, which is a measure of statistical dependence between the rankings of two variables, here children's years of schooling and parents' years of schooling. The higher the correlation, the more strongly parents' educational rank predicts their children's educational rank. See box 3.4 for details.

Conflict's Impact on Labor Market Outcomes

People's human capital (health and education) enables them to get jobs, earn money, build assets, and contribute to national economic progress. The labor market is the platform that lets people translate their knowledge and skills into economic productivity and earnings. To understand how FCS affect welfare and national development prospects over time, a fundamental question is how conflict influences labor market outcomes. To date, however, very few studies have assessed the impact of conflict on long-run labor market results.

Among those that have, the limited evidence points to lasting harms. Galdo (2013), for example, assesses the impact of fetal, early childhood, and preschool exposure to the Peruvian civil war of 1980 to 1995 on labor market outcomes in adulthood. He finds that exposure to the conflict during individuals' first three years of life reduced their labor earnings in adulthood, as well as the probability of working in formal jobs and the probability of working in large firms. However, the same effect was not observed among those exposed in utero or during their preschool year. The analysis suggests that long-run impacts unfolded through the human capital channel, in particular, through irreversible health deterioration in a critical phase for human capital accumulation, and to a lesser degree through reduced schooling and household wealth.[9]

The scant available evidence suggests that, along with its broad devastation, conflict may bring collateral labor-market benefits for some groups under certain conditions. For example, a handful of studies report increased labor market participation for women in some conflict and postconflict settings.[10] However, where increased labor market participation has been reported it is often in low-skill jobs in the informal sector (Ibáñez and Moya 2006; Justino and Verwimp 2013). Little evidence is available about the impact of female labor force participation on household welfare in these settings (Justino 2018).

Impact on Productive Assets and Income-Earning Activities

In addition to conflict's human capital impacts, it is intuitively clear that warfare harms people's economic prospects by destroying or damaging household productive assets and disrupting economic activity. Research supports the intuitive view for short-term effects, while long-term impacts remain largely unstudied.

There is clear evidence that conflict has immediate negative impacts on household assets, including productive assets and those used for coping with adverse income shocks. In low-income countries, livestock and other farm assets often represent most of a rural household's savings and productive assets (Blattman and Miguel 2010). According to Verpoorten (2009), the 1994 Rwandan genocide was associated with a 50 percent loss in cattle.[11] Likewise, the literature reports substantial losses in cattle and other assets, including houses, during conflict episodes, for instance in Mozambique (Brück 2001), Tajikistan (Shemyakina 2011), and Burundi (Verwimp and Van Bavel 2013). Related to this pattern is evidence provided by Deininger (2003) that Uganda's civil conflict during the 1990s reduced household enterprise investment and start-up of nonfarm enterprises, while also increasing rates of failure among such firms.

Amodio, Baccini, and Di Maio (2017) show that conflict during the Second Intifada in Palestine led to distortions in the functioning and accessibility of markets for production inputs, inducing firms to substitute domestically produced materials for imported ones. These distortions explain over 70 percent of the drop in the output value of firms in high-conflict districts. The authors suggest that such distortions are one of the drivers of the negative relationship between conflict and aggregate economic activity observed in the short term. However, researchers have not yet systematically studied whether asset losses and negative impacts on entrepreneurship translate into welfare losses in the long run. The question of what types of asset losses are most damaging for households and firms also remains open.

What is clear, meanwhile, is that household asset destruction can exacerbate damage to human capital. For example, initial evidence provided by Minoiu and Shemyakina (2014) shows that economic losses were an important mechanism in explaining the decline in child health in the context of conflict in Côte d'Ivoire. If a household experienced the destruction of productive assets such as livestock or properties such as farms, the negative impact of conflict on child health was more pronounced. A similar pattern was seen with loss of employment and generally with a fall in household revenues. Affected households and communities may struggle to escape from the resulting destructive cycles. To break the downward spiral, the authors propose targeted interventions aimed at rebuilding household assets in conflict regions, for instance through cash transfers and employment programs. An assessment of policy responses to asset losses resulting from violent conflicts might provide evidence on the circumstances in which these impacts persist and identify effective counter-interventions.

With regard to firms, Collier and Duponchel (2013) provide evidence for persistent negative postconflict impacts of violent conflict in the context of the Sierra Leone civil war from 1991 to 2002. The authors find that entrepreneurs in areas where the conflict was more intense are more willing to pay for staff training, suggesting more severe scarcity of skilled labor. The underlying mechanism proposed by the authors is that the disruptions induced by civil war reduce the maintenance of skills. As a result of violent conflict, workers confront major technical regress; for instance, lack of electricity might result in the use of production practices that would be inefficient in peacetime. Further, a conflict-induced lack of demand reduces employment possibilities. In both cases, workers forget more efficient techniques, as they are not using these skills continuously. Such losses to the skills dimension of human capital may have serious consequences for the future viability of firms seeking to operate in the affected areas.

Conflict-Induced Displacement: How Do Refugees Impact Host Communities?

Analyses of the long-term effects of conflict have generally focused on the countries where the main fighting takes place. However, conflict and its impacts frequently spill across borders. One of the clearest examples is forced population displacement following outbreaks of violence, which can evolve into a chronic challenge for neighboring countries if conflict is prolonged.

Countries that receive large populations fleeing from conflict are concerned about effects on the local population and economy. So far, there is very little rigorous research on the impacts of refugee arrivals on host communities in developing countries. However, three papers have assessed the impact of the 1993–4 refugee inflows from Burundi and Rwanda on the host population in Tanzania (Alix-Garcia and Saah 2010; Baez 2011; and Maystadt and Verwimp 2014). These studies consider different outcomes and offer varying pictures of the impact of the refugee influx on hosts' welfare.

Alix-Garcia and Saah (2010), for example, looked at changes in food prices and measures of household wealth among hosts following the refugees' arrival. They found that prices for agricultural products not covered by food aid increased, while the presence of food aid had only modest negative effects on the prices of agricultural products covered in the aid package. They also detected positive wealth effects for nearby rural households following the arrival of refugees, along with negative wealth effects for urban households. This is probably because local rural households producing food benefited from price increases, while consumer households were disadvantaged. Maystadt and Verwimp (2014) studied the impact of the same refugee influx on welfare measured as consumption. Their research shows a positive aggregate effect of the arrival of refugees on the welfare of the local Tanzanian population. In other words, on average, host households fared better economically following the refugee influx. But not all households benefited. While self-employed farmers could profit from the supply of cheap labor, agricultural workers suffered from increased labor market competition and higher prices in the goods market. Likewise, those self-employed in nonagricultural activities saw their welfare deteriorate, which the authors explain with increased competition from refugee entrepreneurs.

Meanwhile, Baez (2011) focused specifically on the impact of the refugee inflow on local Tanzanian children. The study assessed short- and long-term effects. On the one hand, it presents quasi-experimental evidence for a negative impact on health outcomes in the short run. The incidence of infectious diseases increased, under-five mortality rose, and children's anthropometrics worsened. Moreover, 10 years after the refugee influx, the study found persistent negative impacts on height in early adulthood, on schooling, and on literacy in the local population.

Thus, the limited evidence available suggests a mixed picture. Studies like that of Baez (2011) warn of potentially lasting human capital losses among some host populations in developing countries that receive refugees. Other studies find much more modest negative effects, or report actual welfare gains that can accrue to host communities when refugees arrive. In some contexts, and for some segments of host populations, such benefits appear to outweigh any negative impacts (box 3.5). More research in developing countries is needed to comprehensively assess the effects of large refugee inflows in these host environments in the long run.

Can Refugees Boost Welfare among Host Populations? Evidence from the Syrian Crisis

An emerging literature has assessed the impact of Syrian refugees on the main neighboring host countries, focusing primarily on labor market impacts and considering short-term results. Two papers study the impact of the influx of Syrian refugees into Turkey. Ceritoglu et al. (2015) find that, while refugees displaced native workers in the informal sector, they do not necessarily lower native wages. Del Carpio and Wagner (2015) show that the lower cost of production from cheaper migrant labor induced displaced Turkish workers to upgrade their jobs. Therefore, while some native workers in the informal sector were displaced, particularly women and persons without any formal education, others adjusted by moving from informal to formal jobs. These results are consistent with findings in the United States and suggest that the informal sector in a middle-income economy could have the capacity to absorb the labor of forced migrants by inducing native workers to upgrade their skills.

Furthermore, these studies suggest that restricting refugees from the formal labor market only exaggerates the negative effects that refugees can have on host countries (Del Carpio and Wagner 2015; Fakih and Ibrahim 2016). Meanwhile, for Syrian refugees in Lebanon, Lehmann and Masterson (2014) show that humanitarian aid to refugees can support local economies by increasing demand at local businesses. By far the largest share of cash grants to refugees is spent in the town where they reside.

Adding It All Up: Conflict Imposes Heavy Costs that Extend to Future Generations

The destructive economic and welfare impacts of conflict continue after the fighting stops, compromising development and poverty reduction in the long term. While knowledge gaps remain, the evidence reviewed in this section supports clear conclusions. Through its lasting impacts on human capital—health, cognitive development, educational attainment, and workers' skills—conflict today will continue to inflict heavy welfare losses into the future. When a country's physical assets are destroyed by fighting, they can in theory be replaced. But by compromising human capital, conflict attacks the very roots of resilience and economic competitivity in individuals and nations.

In light of conflict's enduring negative impact on welfare and economic development, policy action to address the challenges of FCS is critical. Policy must focus above all on conflict prevention, but also encompass measures for mitigation and recovery. But what policies will work?

Given the vast differences among countries classified as FCS, no uniform solutions can be expected. But this cannot mean that there are no meaningful commonalities among groups of countries in FCS, and that policy making must start from zero in each new setting. On the contrary, we can assume that such potentially useful commonalities exist. The problem is to find them. The next chapter proposes a data-driven approach to classifying countries at risk of experiencing FCS, based on characteristics that may be amenable to policy intervention. This is a modest step toward generating tools that may ultimately help tailor policies more effectively to countries' needs.

Notes

1. Some researchers have done cross-country comparisons. See, for example, Cerra and Saxena (2008), Collier and Hoeffler (2004), and Elbadawi et al. (2008). Cross-country studies suffer from problems of endogeneity and often include very heterogeneous conflict experiences, further complicating interpretation. See Blattman and Miguel (2010) for a comprehensive review. More recent studies have emphasized microdata and specific country cases. Examples include Acemoglu, Hassan, and Robinson (2011) and Miguel and Roland (2011).

2. The contrasting findings of Miguel and Roland (2011) and Acemoglu, Hassan, and Robinson (2011) are illustrative. Assessing the long-run district-level economic impact of U.S. bombings during the Vietnam War, Miguel and Roland conclude that, 30 years after the conflict, the Vietnamese districts affected by bombings had recovered in terms of output, consumption, infrastructure, poverty, literacy, and population density. In contrast, Acemoglu, Hassan, and Robinson, studying long-term economic and political impacts of the Holocaust in Russia, found a persistent negative correlation between the intensity of the Holocaust and economic outcomes. Decades after the war, per capita income and average wages were also negatively associated with the local intensity of the Holocaust.

3. For Burundi, Bundervoet, Verwimp, and Akresh (2007) and Bundervoet and Verwimp (2005) establish a negative effect of the country's civil war on the height-for-age of affected children. Further evidence on the negative impact of conflict on child health, proxied by child stature, is provided for Rwanda by Akresh, Verwimp, and Bundervoet (2011). Whereas most of the literature on developing countries examines internal conflicts, Akresh, Lucchetti, and Thirumurthy (2012) assess the impact of a conflict between countries, in the 1998–2000 Eritrean-Ethiopian war, on health outcomes in Eritrea. In line with the literature on internal conflicts, the authors find that children born before or during the war experienced a reduction in their height-for-age z-scores as a consequence of conflict exposure. Mansour and Rees (2012) find that, in the context of the al-Aqsa Intifada, intrauterine exposure to armed conflict is negatively associated with the risk of having a low-birth-weight child. Ekhator-Mobayode and Abebe Asfaw (2019) compare child health indicators in areas of Nigeria heavily affected by the Boko Haram insurgency versus mildly affected areas. They report reduced weight-for-age and weight-for-height z-scores and higher probability of wasting among children in areas where Boko Haram was highly active. Some studies trace such patterns forward chronologically into children's adolescence and adulthood. For example, Akresh et al. (2012), studying the 1967–70 Nigerian civil war, found that children and adolescents subjected to the conflict showed reduced average adult stature.

4. Since the labor market outcomes are measured at the individual level, the authors note that the findings may constitute an upper bound of the corresponding effects at the household level, given the potential use of coping strategies to deal with the negative impact of adverse health shocks on household income experienced by an individual member (for instance, other household members might subsequently increase their labor supply).

5. An exception is the work of Valente (2013), who studies the impact of the Nepalese civil conflict and finds increases in female educational attainment as a result of higher conflict intensity. Valente suggests that the puzzling positive impact found may be very context-specific and reflect some Maoists' efforts to remove educational barriers for women. On the other hand, Maoist groups sometimes targeted school children for abduction, and children who suffered abduction had lower subsequent educational attainment.

6. In the context of Guatemala's 36-year civil war, Chamarbagwala and Morán (2011) also report negative effects for rural Mayan males and females who were of primary school age during the conflict. Primary school outcomes among rural Mayan males and females who were of school age in the postwar period improved, however, suggesting that a comparatively rapid postwar recovery benefited subsequent cohorts.

7. Most of the literature that assesses the impact of conflict on education uses difference-in-difference identification strategies that exploit the variation in conflict location and birth cohorts.

8. Another strategy could be to control for potential confounding factors, particularly the log of gross domestic product (GDP) per capita, which is known to be related to intergenerational mobility (Narayan et al. 2018). When controlling for log GDP per capita, there remains a negative relationship between absolute mobility and conflict deaths per 100,000, but the coefficient on conflict deaths is halved in size. With regard to intergenerational persistence, the coefficient on conflict deaths is reduced by two-thirds when controlling for log GDP per capita, but remains positive.

9. Focusing on a specific affected constituency, Blattman and Annan (2010) study labor market outcomes among involuntarily recruited former child soldiers in Uganda. The researchers find that abduction reduced schooling, literacy, and wages. Furthermore, although former child soldiers are as likely to be working as are nonabductees, they work in lower-skilled and less capital-intensive jobs.

10. For example, Shemyakina (2015) assesses the long-term impact of the 1992–98 armed conflict in Tajikistan on labor market outcomes. While she does not find an impact on wages, the conflict increased female labor force participation eight years after the conflict. In Nepal, Menon and van der Meulen Rodgers (2015) report a similar added-worker effect of women joining the labor force to compensate for declines in household earnings due to conflict-related disruptions, injuries, or death. However, Menon and van der Meulen Rodgers assess only the short-run impact of the Nepali conflict.

11. Cattle were perceived as an important war trophy and associated with the ethnic identity of the population targeted during the 1994 genocide in Rwanda (Verpoorten 2009). During the genocide, cattle prices plummeted, making cattle sales an ineffective strategy for coping with soaring food prices, and households targeted during the genocide were not able to access markets and sell their cattle, because it was risky for them to travel.

References

Acemoglu, D., T. A. Hassan, and J. A. Robinson. 2011. "Social Structure and Development: A legacy of the Holocaust in Russia." *Quarterly Journal of Economics* 126 (2): 895–946.

Akresh, R., S. Bhalotra, M. Leone, and U. O. Osili. 2012. "War and Stature: Growing up during the Nigerian Civil War." *American Economic Review* 102 (3): 273–77.

Akresh, R., S. Bhalotra, M. Leone, and U. O. Osili. 2018. "First and Second Generation Impacts of the Biafran War." Working Paper 23721, National Bureau of Economic Research, Cambridge, MA.

Akresh, R., and D. de Walque. 2008. "Armed Conflict and Schooling: Evidence from the 1994 Rwandan Genocide." Working Paper 47, Households in Conflict Network, Brighton, UK.

Akresh, R., L. Lucchetti, and H. Thirumurthy. 2012. "Wars and Child Health: Evidence from the Eritrean–Ethiopian Conflict." *Journal of Development Economics* 99 (2): 330–40.

Akresh, R., P. Verwimp, and T. Bundervoet. 2011. "Civil War, Crop Failure, and Child Stunting in Rwanda." *Economic Development and Cultural Change* 59 (4): 777–810.

Alderman, H., J. Hoddinott, and B. Kinsey. 2006. "Long-Term Consequences of Early Childhood Malnutrition." *Oxford Economic Papers* 58 (3): 450–74.

Alix-Garcia, Jennifer, and David Saah. 2010. "Effect of Refugee Inflows on Host Communities: Evidence from Tanzania." *World Bank Economic Review* 24 (1): 148–70.

Amodio, Francesco, Leonardo Baccini, and Michele Di Maio. 2017. "Security, Trade, and Political Violence." Discussion Paper 10819, Institute for the Study of Labor (IZA), Bonn, Germany. https://ssrn.com/abstract=2988166.

Baez, J. E. 2011. "Civil Wars beyond Their Borders: The Human Capital and Health Consequences of Hosting Refugees." *Journal of Development Economics* 96 (2): 391–408.

Barro, R.J., and X. Sala-i-Martin. 2004. *Economic Growth*. 2nd Edition. Cambridge, MA: MIT Press.

Bertoni, E., M. Di Maio, V. Molini, and R. Nistico. 2019. "Education Is Forbidden: The Effect of the Boko Haram Conflict on Education in North-East Nigeria." *Journal of Development Economics* 141 (C): 102–249.

Blattman, C., and J. Annan. 2010. "The Consequences of Child Soldiering." *Review of Economics and Statistics*, 92 (4): 882–98.

Blattman, Christopher, and Edward Miguel. 2010. "Civil War." *Journal of Economic Literature* 48 (1): 3–57.

Bossavie, Laurent, Harold Alderman, John Giles, and Cem Mete. 2017. "The Effect of Height on Earnings: Is Stature Just a Proxy for Cognitive and Non-Cognitive Skills?" Policy Research Working Paper 8254, World Bank, Washington, DC.

Bratti, M., M. Mendolab, and A. Mirandac. 2016. "Hard to Forget: The Long-Lasting Impact of War on Mental Health." HiCN Working Paper 206, Households in Conflict Network, Brighton, UK.

Brück, T. 2001. "Coping with Peace: Post-War Household Strategies in Northern Mozambique." PhD thesis, Oxford University, UK.

Bundervoet, T., and S. Fransen. 2018. "The Educational Impact of Shocks in Utero: Evidence from Rwanda." *Economics and Human Biology* 29: 88–101.

Bundervoet, T., and P. Verwimp. 2005. "Civil War and Economic Sanctions: Analysis of Anthropometric Outcomes in Burundi." HiCN Working Paper 11, Households in Conflict Network, Brighton, UK.

Bundervoet, T., P. Verwimp, and R. Akresh. 2007. "Health and Civil War in Rural Burundi." Discussion Paper 2951, Institute for the Study of Labor (IZA), Bonn, Germany.

Case, Anne, and Christina Paxson. 2008. "Stature and Status: Height, Ability, and Labor Market Outcomes." *Journal of Political Economy* 116 (3): 499–532.

Ceritoglu, Evren, H. Burcu Gurcihan Yunculer, Huzeyfe Torun, and Semih Tumen. 2015. "The Impact of Syrian Refugees on Natives' Labor Market Outcomes in Turkey: Evidence from a Quasi-Experimental Design." IZA Discussion Paper 9348, Institute for the Study of Labor (IZA), Bonn, Germany.

Cerra, V., and S. C. Saxena. 2008. "Growth Dynamics: The Myth of Economic Recovery." *American Economic Review* 98 (1): 439–57.

Chamarbagwala, R., and H. E. Morán. 2011. "The Human Capital Consequences of Civil War: Evidence from Guatemala." *Journal of Development Economics* 94 (1): 41–61.

Collier, P., and M. Duponchel. 2013. "The Economic Legacy of Civil War: Firm-level Evidence from Sierra Leone." *Journal of Conflict Resolution* 57 (1): 65–88.

Collier, Paul, and Anke Hoeffler. 2004. "Greed and Grievance in Civil War." *Oxford Economic Papers* 56 (4): 563–95.

Dabalen, A. L., and S. Paul. 2014. "Estimating the Effects of Conflict on Education in Côte d'Ivoire." *Journal of Development Studies* 50 (12): 1631–46.

Deininger, K. 2003. "Causes and Consequences of Civil Strife: Micro-Level Evidence from Uganda." *Oxford Economic Papers* 55 (4): 579–606.

Del Carpio, Ximena Vanessa, and Mathis Christoph Wagner. 2015. "The Impact of Syrians Refugees on the Turkish Labor Market." Policy Research Working Paper 7402, World Bank, Washington, DC.

Ekhator-Mobayode, U. E., and A. Abebe Asfaw. 2019. "The Child Health Effects of Terrorism: Evidence from the Boko Haram Insurgency in Nigeria." *Applied Economics* 51 (6): 624–38.

Elbadawi I. A., L., Kaltani, and K. Schmidt-Hebbel. 2008). "Foreign Aid, the Real Exchange Rate, and Economic Growth in the Aftermath of Civil Wars." *World Bank Economic Review* 22 (1): 113–40.

Fakih, A., and M. Ibrahim. 2016. "The Impact of Syrian Refugees on the Labor Market in Neighboring Countries: Empirical Evidence from Jordan." *Defence and Peace Economics* 27 (1): 64–86.

Galdo, J. 2013. "The Long-Run Labor-Market Consequences of Civil War: Evidence from the Shining Path in Peru." *Economic Development and Cultural Change* 61 (4): 789–823.

Global Database on Intergenerational Mobility. 2018. Development Research Group, World Bank. Washington, DC: World Bank Group.

Ibáñez, Ana María, and Andres Moya. 2006. "The Impact of Intra-State Conflict on Economic Welfare and Consumption Smoothing: Empirical Evidence for the Displaced Population in Colombia." HiCN Working Paper 23, Households in Conflict Network, Brighton, UK.

Justino, Patricia. 2018. "Violent Conflict and Changes in Gender Economic Roles: Implications for Post-Conflict Economic Recovery." In *The Oxford Handbook of Gender and Conflict*, edited by Fionnuala Ní Aoláin, Naomi Cahn, Dina Francesca Haynes, and Nahla Valji. Oxford: Oxford Handbooks Online. https://www.oxfordhandbooks.com/view/10.1093/oxfordhb/9780199300983.001.0001 /oxfordhb-9780199300983-e-7.

Justino, Patricia, and Philip Verwimp. 2013. "Poverty Dynamics, Violent Conflict and Convergence in Rwanda." MICROCON Research Working Paper 4. http://dx.doi.org/10.2139/ssrn.1116610.

Kadir, A., S. Shenoda, and J. Goldhagen. 2019. "Effects of Armed Conflict on Child Health and Development: A Systematic Review." *PloS One* 14 (1). https://journals.plos.org/plosone /article?id=10.1371/journal.pone.0210071.

Lehmann, Christian, and Daniel T. R. Masterson. 2014. "Impact Evaluation of a Cash-Transfer Programme for Syrian Refugees in Lebanon." *Field Exchange* 48: 56–62. https://www.ennonline .net/fex/48/impactevaluation.

Mansour, Hani, and Daniel I. Rees. 2012. "Armed Conflict and Birth Weight: Evidence from the al-Aqsa Intifada." *Journal of Development Economics* 99 (1): 190–99.

Maystadt, Jean-François, and Philip Verwimp. 2014. "Winners and Losers among a Refugee-Hosting Population." *Economic Development and Cultural Change* 62 (4): 769–809.

Menon, N., and Y. van der Meulen Rodgers. 2015. "War and Women's Work: Evidence from the Conflict in Nepal." *Journal of Conflict Resolution* 59 (1): 51–73.

Miguel, E., and G. Roland. 2011. "The Long-Run Impact of Bombing Vietnam." *Journal of Development Economics* 96 (1): 1–15.

Minoiu, Camelia, and Olga N. Shemyakina. 2014. "Armed Conflict, Household Victimization, and Child Health in Côte d'Ivoire." *Journal of Development Economics* 108: 237–55.

Narayan, Ambar, Roy Van der Weide, Alexandru Cojocaru, Christoph Lakner, Silvia Redaelli, Daniel Gerszon Mahler, Rakesh Gupta N. Ramasubbaiah, and Stefan Thewissen. 2018. *Fair Progress? Economic Mobility across Generations around the World.* Washington, DC: World Bank.

Phadera, L. 2019. "Unfortunate Moms and Unfortunate Children: Impact of Nepalese Civil War on Women's Stature and Intergenerational Health." Unpublished manuscript.

Pivovarova, M., and E. L. Swee. 2015. "Quantifying the Microeconomic Effects of War Using Panel Data: Evidence from Nepal." *World Development* 66: 308–21.

Schultz, Paul. 2003. "Wage Rentals for Reproductive Human Capital: Evidence from Ghana and the Ivory Coast." *Economics and Human Biology* 1 (3): 331–36.

Shemyakina, O. 2011. "The Effect of Armed Conflict on Accumulation of Schooling: Results from Tajikistan." *Journal of Development Economics* 95 (2): 186–200.

Shemyakina, O. 2015. "Exploring the Impact of Conflict Exposure during Formative Years on Labour Market Outcomes in Tajikistan." *Journal of Development Studies* 51 (4): 422–46.

Singh, P., and O. N. Shemyakina. 2016. "Gender-Differential Effects of Terrorism on Education: The Case of the 1981–1993 Punjab Insurgency." *Economics of Education Review* 54: 185–210.

Singhal, S. (forthcoming). "Early Life Shocks and Mental Health: The Long-Term Effect of War in Vietnam." *Journal of Development Economics.*

Strauss, J., and D. Thomas. 1998. "Health, Nutrition, and Economic Development." *Journal of Economic Literature* 36 (2): 766–817.

Swee, E. L. 2015. "On War Intensity and Schooling Attainment: The Case of Bosnia and Herzegovina." *European Journal of Political Economy* 40: 158–72.

UCDP (Uppsala Conflict Data Program). 2019. *UCDP Conflict Encyclopedia,* accessed July 1, 2019. Sweden: Department of Peace and Conflict Research, Uppsala University. https://www.ucdp.uu.se.

Valente, C. 2013. "Education and Civil Conflict in Nepal." *World Bank Economic Review* 28 (2): 354–83.

Verpoorten, M. 2009. "Household Coping in War- and Peacetime: Cattle Sales in Rwanda, 1991–2001." *Journal of Development Economics* 88 (1): 67-86.

Verwimp, P., and J. Van Bavel. 2013. "Schooling, Violent Conflict, and Gender in Burundi." *World Bank Economic Review* 28 (2): 384–411.

Wagner, Zachary, Sam Heft-Neal, Zulfiqar A. Bhutta, Robert E. Black, Marshall Burke, and Eran Bendavid. 2018. "Armed Conflict and Child Mortality in Africa: A Geospatial Analysis." *Lancet* 392: 857–65.

World Bank. 2018. "The Human Capital Project." World Bank, Washington, DC. https://www.worldbank.org/en/publication/human-capital.

4. Patterns of Fragility—Understanding Diversity in Country Profiles

Key Messages

- *To tailor policy solutions for fragile and conflict-affected situations (FCS), decision makers need a data-driven typology of current FCS.*
- *An in-depth understanding of the complexity of fragility would help identify countries for priority preventive action and for differentiated interventions.*
- *We propose a data-driven set of country fragility profiles, using latent mixture analysis based on governance, conflict, and socioeconomic variables.*
- *The analysis suggests that monitoring select fragility markers may enable some countries not in FCS to implement better preemptive strategies.*

Introduction

Previous sections underscored important commonalities across FCS economies regarding poverty and welfare. For example, most economies in FCS have high rates of monetary poverty, on average substantially exceeding rates in non-FCS. Poor people in most FCS are also more likely than the poor elsewhere to experience deprivation in nonmonetary domains, and thus to face multiple forms of deprivation simultaneously. Furthermore, the length of exposure to fragile and conflict conditions systematically worsens these welfare outcomes. Finally, a growing body of evidence documents that exposure to conflict results in intergenerational deficits in human capital, contributing to long-term poverty traps. Such common traits across fragile and conflict-affected settings combined with the chronic nature of FCS explain the steady rise in the share of the global poor who live in FCS.

Alongside shared characteristics, however, countries in FCS exhibit marked diversity. For example, they include both countries plunged in prolonged high-intensity conflict and others that have rarely or never experienced armed conflict per se but whose institutions are weak for other reasons. Heterogeneity in FCS poses challenges for policy, making it difficult to formulate general principles for addressing fragility or to gauge whether lessons from one economy in FCS may apply to others. Decision makers need a framework for understanding the heterogeneity of FCS that can guide a differentiated policy and programming approach for more effective solutions.

This chapter attempts to explore patterns of fragility in a way that can inform policy choices in all countries, including but not limited to current FCS. It aims to uncover markers of fragility that may deserve active monitoring in all contexts. To do so, the chapter uses information for 189 countries and applies an empirical approach underpinned by a wide range of data on the characteristics of economies classified as FCS and those that may be vulnerable to fragility.

It is important to note that the clustering analysis described here does not furnish a means to predict conflict or fragility outcomes in individual countries. Accurately predicting conflict in a specific country context requires incorporating the many social, economic, political, and other factors that may push a country into an outbreak of violence or maintain an otherwise fragile environment without major violence. Relevant factors are often hard to identify and harder still to measure. Moreover, a country's specific history of fragility and violence plays a role in its propensity for and pathways into conflict. Predicting any individual country's future trajectory with regard to fragility and conflict is an uncertain exercise at best and beyond the scope of this book.

The analysis proposed here has other aims. One is to demonstrate the heterogeneity that can be observed in country fragility profiles. Building on that result, a second objective is to detect and differentiate markers of fragility that, while they do not imply individualized predictions, can help decision makers anticipate fragility trends and act preemptively to address specific underlying factors. By better understanding both differences and similarities across country groupings, countries can more readily identify policy options likely to prove effective in their respective situations. Monitoring markers of fragility systematically can help improve country diagnostics and identify priorities with a view to mitigating adverse welfare impacts.

Cluster Analysis for Creating Country Typologies

The causes of fragility and conflict are multiple and often elusive. As the United Nations and World Bank (2018) publication *Pathways for Peace* notes, the best predictor of violence is past violence. Idiosyncratic, country-specific factors and events often tip the balance from relative stability to instability, or from economic and political fragility to full-blown conflict. While it is often impossible to predict a specific country's trajectory into or away from FCS, it is feasible to create a typology that establishes empirical distinctions across groups of countries while highlighting shared features within each group.[1]

To consider the criteria such a typology might include, one can begin with the formal definition of FCS currently used by the World Bank Group. This definition is based on four measures: (a) the intensity of conflict, (b) the level of institutional fragility as measured by Country Policy and Institutional Assessment (CPIA) scores, (c) the

Fragility and Conflict

presence of United Nations peacekeeping operations, or (d) the number of refugees originating from the country.[2] Matching under any of these criteria results in an economy being classified as FCS for that year. The most recent World Bank FCS list includes 37 economies.

The World Bank's criteria for FCS have changed over time, and other approaches to characterizing fragility have been proposed in the academic literature.[3] Indeed, there is no consensus definition of "state fragility." Several organizations have developed different methodologies to create fragility indices and arrived at different country rankings: for example, the State Fragility Index from the Center for Systemic Peace (Marshall and Elzinga-Marshall 2017),[4] the Fragile States Index published by the Fund for Peace (2019),[5] and the Organisation for Economic Co-operation and Development's States of Fragility (OECD 2018).[6] The best-known classification schemes currently identify some 30 to 40 fragile states, some of which are not conflict affected.

Poor governance and weak institutions are widely seen as key contributors to fragility. However, governance structures do not exist in isolation from other features of society that may encourage fragility and conflict. Recent studies have found that weak institutions combined with poor welfare outcomes can create fragility and risk of conflict. Conservatively put, weak governance can at least be viewed as a precursor symptom that signals an elevated risk of fragility (Ferreira 2015; World Bank 2017).[7]

The remainder of this chapter aims to show that data-driven methods incorporating multiple variables can simultaneously (a) distinguish subgroups of countries by policy-relevant differences and (b) uncover common markers of fragility that may guide shared learning and support evidence-based action.

To introduce the analysis, the following section considers a range of fragility markers and proposes a clustering approach to identify country typologies.

An Empirical Approach to Exploring Patterns of Fragility

We follow previous studies to arrive at a data-driven clustering of countries (see Ferreira 2015; Grävingholt, Ziaja, and Kreibaum 2012). Given the relative consensus on the role of governance in fragility, we create groups based on governance indicators,[8] along with other salient markers identified in the literature, that closely match the criteria used by the World Bank Group and other organizations in developing fragility classifications.

The clustering approach taken here (box 4.1) is the same as that used by Grävingholt, Ziaja, and Kreibaum (2012): latent mixture models (box 4.2). Clustering models group countries according to their observed characteristics, not by preset definitions. In other words, in clustering, one does not need to specify the criteria for fragile situations in advance in order to group countries. Clustering lets the most relevant criteria for grouping emerge from the data itself, and is not a prediction tool.

Clustering in Action

Many people have had the experience of receiving online product recommendations, whether for a movie on a video streaming platform or an item for purchase on a shopping site. In such situations, we may sometimes have wondered why the platform was trying to interest us in these particular products. Behind the recommendations are clustering algorithms. Based on a consumer's characteristics and previous viewing or shopping patterns, the algorithm recognizes a similarity to a group of other customers. Drawing on previous choices made by members of the group, the algorithm then recommends a new product for the consumer to consider.

Clustering is an approach that divides items into groups based on similarity. In the shopping example, the items being grouped are people—customers. The approach in this case is predicated on a simple idea. Because your purchase history and demographics are similar to those of other people who have bought a certain product, you may also want to buy that product.

Today, clustering techniques are also being used to guide much more important decisions. For instance, clustering algorithms are emerging as powerful tools in medicine. Patients presumed to be suffering from the same disease often display wide heterogeneity in their symptoms and may respond very differently to the same treatment. Cluster analysis can improve diagnostic accuracy and help doctors understand why some patients respond well to a given treatment while others do not. This can contribute to designing personalized medical therapies (Windgassen et al. 2018).

The clustering approach yields groups that are not defined a priori and are mutually exclusive and collectively exhaustive over the set of countries for which data are available. In brief, this approach maximizes within-group similarity and across-group dissimilarities. Since this is a statistical model, there is a degree of uncertainty attached to a country's membership in a group or, to put it positively, a degree of confidence to the assignment. The ideal number of groups is not defined beforehand and is usually driven by different measures of how well the data fit the number of groups.

The clustering described here is conducted with the following set of variables and data sources:[9]

- *Voice and accountability* measures the extent to which a country's citizens are able to participate in selecting their government and to enjoy freedom of expression, freedom of association, and a free media. Data source: Worldwide Governance Indicators (WGI).
- *Political stability and absence of violence* measures perceptions of the likelihood of political instability and/or politically motivated violence, including terrorism. Data source: WGI.
- *Government effectiveness* captures perceptions of the quality of civil service and the degree of its independence from political pressures, the quality of policy formulation and implementation, and the credibility of the government's commitment to such policies. Data source: WGI.

Mixture Models: Latent Profile Analysis

As machine learning has gained prominence, so too has the popularity of clustering and classification methods. The application of such approaches to the issues of fragility and conflict is not new. This study is similar to previous work by researchers including Grävingholt, Ziaja, and Kreibaum (2012) and Ferreira (2015).

Approaches like the one presented in this chapter, clustering, differ from other methods in a fundamental respect: clustering-type approaches are not based on criteria set in advance, before engaging with the data. A clustering procedure can be applied when we start with a large set of items (for example, countries) and we believe that different types of groups exist within that large set yet we lack knowledge of what these groups may be, or which observations belong to the different groups. As an example, Ferreira (2015) relied on hierarchical cluster analysis to create mutually exclusive groups that are similar to one another according to a defined criterion and dissimilar to other groups. The method avoids having to impose preconceived values in order to create groups. It allows the data to "tell" the investigators what the relevant groups are.

Like hierarchical clustering, latent profile analysis is a statistical technique that helps uncover groupings that are not overtly present in the data. It is a model-based alternative to clustering algorithms, one that can outperform more traditional clustering techniques, for example, K-means (see Magidson and Vermunt 2002). The method has useful properties that we exploit in this analysis, including a measure of uncertainty of group membership, and allowing for counterfactual tests.

A simple illustration of the latent profile method is presented by Oberski (2016). It can be explained by supposing we have a data set with a vector of heights for men and women. When graphing the distribution of heights, one can observe two separate peaks. Now imagine that we obtained the data in a statistical office's safe room and forgot to add the variable for the gender, and that we are currently working elsewhere and cannot get the indicator. We know that there is a grouping in our data, and that this is the reason why we have two humps in the distribution: it is actually two separate distributions, one for men and one for women. Latent profile analysis allows us to uncover the hidden grouping.

The problem can be summarized as having to find the means and standard deviations of each distribution. This is done in a somewhat iterative manner, where the process begins with a guess for these parameters and assigns a posterior probability to an observation regarding whether that observation is a man or a woman. The posterior distribution parameters are then used to update the next iteration. This is called the expectation maximization algorithm. This process of iteration is continued until convergence is achieved. In this example, it is possible to see that the distributions of men and women overlap, and thus obtaining the gender of all observations could be complicated. However, as additional variables are introduced to fine tune the process, a clearer demarcation of the hidden group can be obtained.

- *Battle deaths by population** (five-year average) reports battle deaths per million population in the country. Data sources: Armed Conflict Location and Event Data Project (ACLED)[10] and Uppsala Conflict Data Program (UCDP).[11]
- *Refugee population** (five-year average) is self-explanatory. Data sources: World Development Indicators (WDI) and United Nations High Commissioner for Refugees.[12]

- *Homicides per 100,000 population** (five-year average) is self-explanatory. Data source: United Nations Office on Drugs and Crime.
- *Ethnic fractionalization* levels reflect the likelihood that two randomly selected individuals from a given population come from the same ethnic group. Data source: Alesina et al. 2003.[13]
- *Share of gross domestic product (GDP) from natural resources* is the sum of oil rents, natural gas rents, coal rents (hard and soft), mineral rents, and forest rents. Data source: WDI.

This exercise uses data for 189 countries and considers all these dimensions simultaneously in determining country clusters (see appendix E). The result yields six clusters of countries, with groups ranging in size from 3 to 69 countries.[14]

While all these dimensions cannot be simultaneously visualized, some of the two-way correlations can be illustrated. Figure 4.1 presents two-way scatter plots for some select indicators as they emerge from the cluster analysis. For instance, panel a shows

FIGURE 4.1 Scatter Plots for Select Dimensions Used in Clustering Countries

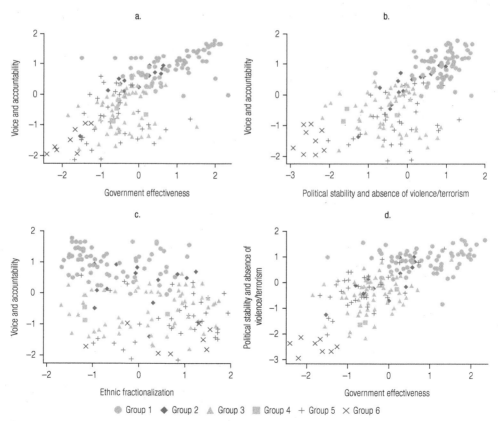

Sources: Based on WGI. See https://info.worldbank.org/governance/wgi/. Ethnic fractionalization data are from Alesina et al. (2003). Values have been standardized to mean 0 and standard deviation of 1.

Fragility and Conflict

a high degree of overlap in voice and accountability and government effectiveness for group 1 in green circles. Voice and accountability and ethnic fractionalization, on the other hand (panel c), have no clear relation: the different country groups that have emerged from the clustering overlap substantially, with no clear splits in the ethnic fractionalization space. The two-way scatter plots also illustrate the robust correlation among the governance indicators.

Country Typologies

To arrange the clusters of countries obtained in the previous step, a governance index is constructed using all six of the Worldwide Governance Indicators.[15] The governance index is used solely for the purpose of ordering the country clusters, from the cluster with the highest group median governance index (group 1) to that with the lowest governance index (group 6). For the six groups, figure 4.2 presents the average value for each of the indicators used in the classification. Values for the indicators are expressed as standard deviations away from the global average. The total number of countries that can be clustered is 189. The countries not included have one or more of the included indicators missing, so they cannot be assigned to a group.

As previously observed by Grävingholt, Ziaja, and Kreibaum (2012), an exercise of this type shows why trying to summarize fragility in a single score is not recommended. In a single index, high values in one dimension may offset low values on a separate dimension. Nuances around why a country is fragile are also lost in an index that presents a single score. One may end up with countries that have similar scores but for very different reasons.

The clusters obtained in the analysis show clear intergroup differences. What makes one group different from the others? One way to answer this question is to obtain defining characteristic(s) for each group and investigate which countries within the group most strongly exhibit that characteristic (or set of characteristics). To accomplish this, we conduct a pairwise comparison of means using Tukey's test (Tukey 1949). This approach is similar to that used by the OECD (2018) to identify salient indicators in their clusters.

Salient characteristics for each group are defined as those for which the average for the group is significantly different from that of at least four other groups. Using this criterion, the following salient characteristics emerge:

- Group 1: Voice and accountability, political stability and absence of violence, and government effectiveness
- Group 2: Voice and accountability, homicides per 100,000 people
- Group 3: No salient characteristic
- Group 4: Refugee population in proportion to total population
- Group 5: Share of GDP from natural resources

FIGURE 4.2 Cluster Means for Indicators

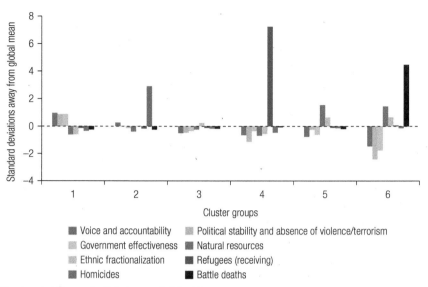

Source: Based on clustering results. Refer to appendix D for data sources.

- Group 6: Share of GDP from natural resources, battle deaths by population, government effectiveness, voice and accountability, and political stability and absence of violence

While the clustering approach proposed in this chapter selects sets of countries based on their similarity along certain statistical characteristics, it is not intended for detailed country-by-country diagnostics or comparisons. Instead, it provides broad guidelines to complement country-level diagnostics and, for some clusters, identifies concrete markers of fragility that characterize the group. For this reason, country examples are not extensively discussed in this section. Detailed consideration of specific countries would instead be most appropriate in the development of a country-based diagnostic tool.

Every group has at least one salient characteristic, with the exception of group 3. Group 3's defining characteristic is that it is the most "average" of the groups, that is, the one least clearly demarcated from others across the six indicators. The relationship between the indicators and the governance index used to order the groups is also notable. As group numbers rise from 1 through 6, governance index values go down. Thus, group 6 shows poor outcomes for battle deaths along with low values for governance indicators.

Cluster Profiles and Entry Points for Policy

When we look in detail at the six clusters of countries obtained through the analysis, what different fragility profiles emerge among the groups? Might these profiles indicate

Fragility and Conflict

entry points where policy can engage? To answer, we consider the groups in numerical order, shifting group 3 to the end because it requires extended discussion.

Group 1 represents countries that are generally performing well and face few risks associated with fragility. The group comprises 69 economies, many of which are high-income. Group 1 countries have high governance indicators, low battle deaths, and a low share of GDP from natural resources. The cluster includes many OECD countries, as well as several small Pacific Island nations that are characterized by institutional fragility.[16] Strengthening economic fundamentals and institutional capacity, particularly in small states, is a priority for countries in this cluster.

Group 2 stands out because of elevated homicide rates, considerably higher than those of any other cluster. Many group 2 countries, such as República Bolivariana de Venezuela, also perform at below-average levels on governance. Tackling safety and security, with strengthened rule of law, transparency, and accountability, is a priority in group 2 countries—recognizing that the underlying causes of heightened homicide and crime vary by country and success will depend substantially on conducive country governance.

Group 4, comprising Lebanon, West Bank and Gaza, and Jordan, is characterized by a particularly high share of refugees, a low share of GDP from natural resources, and the second-lowest value for political stability and absence of violence (see figure 4.2). In addition, all three jurisdictions have relatively low values for the three governance indicators included in the analysis. While hosting a high refugee population is the defining characteristic of this group (the three jurisdictions exhibit the highest shares reported globally), there is no evidence that this factor poses fragility risks. Instead, this group highlights potential risks associated with neighborhood effects, especially those associated with protracted displacement.

Group 5 includes 34 countries and stands out due to a higher-than-average share of GDP derived from natural resources and above-average ethnic fractionalization. This group includes a number of countries that are typically associated with fragility in many models. Countries in this group display a combination of high resource rents, weak governance, and high potential for polarization. The 34 countries in group 5 are among the world's 40 most natural-resource-dependent economies. Engagement in these economies is not necessarily focused on aid, given their high resource rents. However, the group's comparatively poor indicators on voice and accountability and government effectiveness suggest that ensuring broad, equitable distribution of benefits from natural resource rents is both urgent and challenging.

Chad illustrates the difficulties many group 5 countries face in this respect. In the early 2000s, the World Bank attempted to tie oil revenues to poverty reduction in Chad as part of a package to help the country develop its oil industry (Barma et al. 2011). Subsequently, however, few public resources have been allocated to pro-poor spending. As a result, while oil revenues have fueled public consumption and investment in Chad since 2003 (World Bank 2015), to date only a small share of the country's population benefits from the oil bonanza. Results also depend on political support and associated governance arrangements: for example, Guyana (also in group 5) is establishing a wealth fund with the aim that the country's natural resource windfall should benefit the whole population, not just an elite segment of that population.

The most salient characteristic of the countries in group 6 is a high number of battle deaths, along with the lowest governance indicators of all groups. The eight countries in this group rank as the nations with the highest number of battle deaths per 100,000 people. Welfare improvement for the population in this group requires a focus on restoring and rebuilding the citizen-state relationship, strengthening delivery of core state functions, and achieving peace and stability.

Finally, group 3 is made up of 61 countries with some markers of fragility but no clearly distinguishing outlier values. For example, seven of group 3's countries (including Nigeria and Sudan) are among the 20 countries with the highest numbers of conflict-related deaths globally. In the case of Nigeria, conflicts are mostly sub-national. They have worsened recently, as the displacement of herders by Boko Haram has sparked tensions with farmers in neighboring Nigerian states. By some counts, the resulting struggles over resources have already displaced many more people and caused more deaths than the activities of Boko Haram itself (International Crisis Group 2018).

Other group 3 nations that rank among the 20 countries with the highest rates of conflict-related deaths include Ukraine, Cameroon, and Mali. All three also show

FIGURE 4.3 **Country Clusters and Their Shares of the Global Poor, 2000–30**

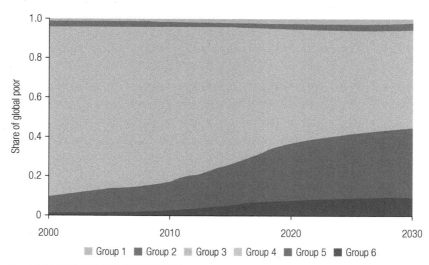

Sources: PovcalNet; UNHCR 2019; IDMC 2019; IMF 2019.

Fragility and Conflict

below-average values for political stability, but perform less poorly on government effectiveness and some other dimensions of governance.[17] Although these countries clearly display a marker of concern with respect to conflict-related deaths, the rates remain well below those of countries in group 6, while no other marker warrants situating these countries in group 6.

Given these examples, group 3 bears watching, as deterioration in some key fragility markers could shift countries' mapping from group 3 to other groups with more immediately alarming fragility profiles. It is also worth noting that, because of the group's size and composition, most of the global poor are concentrated in group 3 countries (figure 4.3). This is another argument for monitoring any shifts in country-level risk profiles and developments within this group.[18]

Conclusions

This chapter has used latent mixture analysis to develop a data-driven country typology of fragility profiles. The typology seeks to reflect the diversity of FCS but also capture policy-relevant common traits among broader subsets of countries. The model does not try to predict conflict. However, by proposing six country fragility profiles with distinctive policy entry points, it may support decision makers in tailoring solutions to different country contexts and highlight areas for monitoring.

This typology alone will not automatically translate into appropriate policy design. Yet in conjunction with other resources, the model can inform action. Building on the fragility profiles and the evidence distilled in earlier chapters, the book's conclusion will map policy directions that countries may consider to advance the frontline struggle against fragility and poverty.

Notes

1. By doing so, within a group composed largely of countries designated as FCS, one may find countries not on the FCS list that appear similar in terms of their fragility profile. These countries may need to be monitored more closely, paying attention to country-specific developments.

2. For a visual presentation of how the World Bank's current FCS criteria are applied, see appendix C.

3. Several studies have focused on identifying symptoms of fragility. For instance, Besley and Persson (2011) explore the origins of fragility and develop a framework in which they posit that the primary symptoms of fragility are state ineffectiveness and political violence. Hence, in their framework, poverty, civil wars, and low income per capita are symptoms of fragility rather than causes. The authors argue that two latent variables that cause fragility are a lack of common interest in the population and a lack of cohesive institutions.

4. The State Fragility Index is an aggregate index of effectiveness and legitimacy scores. It was originally introduced in 2007 (see Marshall and Goldstone 2007), and the authors have made the index comparable across time.

5. The Fragile States Index provides a score based on diverse data sources. These include content analysis of global media, as well as indicator data from the World Bank, United Nations, and others. The data

for each country are also reviewed and assessed based on information that the data may not have captured for the previous year.

6. The OECD's approach relies on hierarchical clustering of countries based on similar characteristics and moves beyond the single index method. The approach yields six groups of countries that are ranked based on their degree of fragility, from severe to nonfragile.

7. Given the gradual and uncertain evolution of institutions, particularly informal institutions, there is no guarantee that formal rules or interventions that were successful in one setting would yield favorable outcomes elsewhere (North 1990). As Rodrik (2008) points out, the question remains which institutions should be reformed and how, which depends on each country's context.

8. Grävingholt, Ziaja, and Kreibaum (2012) use mixture models (cluster analysis) to identify homogenous groups of countries with respect to their chosen indicators. We use a similar approach to infer groupings of countries based on proximity along the indicators adopted here.

9. For variables marked with an asterisk (*), when countries have missing information for a given year, the information is imputed using the previous year's value. Refer to appendix D for more details on data. Variables obtained from the Worldwide Governance Indicators may be found at https://info.worldbank.org/governance/wgi/.

10. ACLED is a disaggregated data collection, analysis, and crisis-mapping project. It collects details about fatalities of all reported political violence and protest events across the globe, with the exception of most high-income countries, as well as Latin America. See https://www .acleddata.com/about-acled/.

11. The UCDP data comes from Uppsala University and has been collected for almost 40 years. It includes data on organized violence and armed conflicts. Annual updates have been published every year since 1993 in the *Journal of Peace Research*. See https://ucdp.uu.se/.

12. Refugee population is not a marker of fragility by itself; rather, it proxies for neighboring conflict with spillovers.

13. Territories for which the indicator was missing (for example, Kosovo, Serbia, South Sudan, Timor-Leste, West Bank and Gaza, and the Republic of Yemen) were completed from different sources. See appendix D for details.

14. The number of clusters is chosen to minimize the Bayes information criterion. This is a common approach to selecting the optimal number of clusters.

15. The governance indicators used for the index are highly correlated, and the index is constructed as a principal component analysis (PCA). The first component of the PCA explains roughly 84 percent of the total variance. Aside from the three WGI governance indicators used for the clustering, we add the remaining three to obtain the PCA: regulatory quality, rule of law, and control of corruption. See appendix E for details.

16. A more in-depth look at these countries reveals that they are performing poorly in the governance indicators not included in the clustering exercise.

17. Ukraine has considerably below-average values for control of corruption and is ranked among the 40 worst global performers in this area.

18. Of note, extreme poverty in group 3 is predicted to fall over time, whereas for countries in groups 5 and 6, it will likely rise.

References

Alesina, A., A. Devleeschauwer, W. Easterly, S. Kurlat, and R. Wacziarg. 2003. "Fractionalization." *Journal of Economic Growth* 8 (2): 155–94.

Barma, N. H., K. Kaiser, T. Minh Le, and L. Vinuela. 2011. *Rents to Riches? The Political Economy of Natural Resource-Led Development*. Washington, DC: World Bank.

Besley, T., and T. Persson. 2011. "Fragile States and Development Policy." *Journal of the European Economic Association* 9 (3). https://doi.org/10.1111/j.1542-4774.2011.01022.x.

Ferreira, I. A. R. 2015. "Defining and Measuring State Fragility: A New Proposal." *Conference Proceedings: The Annual Bank Conference on Africa.* Berkeley, CA.

Grävingholt, J., S. Ziaja, and M. Kreibaum. 2012. "State Fragility: Towards a Multi-Dimensional Empirical Typology." DIE discussion paper 3/2012, SSRN, Rochester, NY. https://ssrn.com/abstract=2279407.

IDMC (International Displacement Monitoring Centre). 2019. Global International Displacement Database (accessed October 15, 2019). http://www.internal-displacement.org/database/displacement-data.

IMF (International Monetary Fund). 2019. World Economic Outlook Database, October 2019 edition (accessed October 15, 2019). https://www.imf.org/external/pubs/ft/weo/2019/02/weodata/index.aspx.

International Crisis Group. 2018. "Stopping Nigeria's Spiraling Farmer-Herder Violence." *International Crisis Group, Africa Report 262.* Brussels: International Crisis Group.

Magidson, J. and J. Vermunt. 2002. "Latent Class Models for Clustering: A Comparison with K-means." *Canadian Journal of Marketing Research* 20 (1): 36–43.

Marshall, M., and G. Elzinga-Marshall. 2017. "Global Report on Conflict, Governance and State Fragility 2017." Vienna, VA: Center for Systemic Peace.

Marshall, M., and J. Goldstone. 2007. "Global Report on Conflict, Governance and State Fragility 2007." *Foreign Policy Bulletin* 17 (S01): 3–21.

North, D. 1990. *Institutions, Institutional Change and Economic Performance.* Cambridge, UK: Cambridge University Press.

Oberski, D. 2016. "Mixture Models: Latent Profile and Latent Class Analysis." In *Modern Statistical Methods for HCI: Human–Computer Interaction Series*, edited by J. Robertson and M. Kaptein, 275–87. Cham, Switzerland: Springer.

OECD (Organisation for Economic Cooperation and Development). 2018. *States of Fragility 2018.* Paris: OECD. https://doi.org/10.1787/9789264302075-en.

Rodrik, Dani. 2008. "Second-Best Institutions." *American Economic Review* 98 (2): 100–4.

Tukey, J. W. 1949. "Comparing Individual Means in the Analysis of Variance." *Biometrics* 5 (2): 99–114.

UNHCR (United Nations High Commissioner for Refugees). 2019. Population Statistics Database (accessed October 15, 2019). http://popstats.unhcr.org/.

United Nations and World Bank. 2018. *Pathways for Peace: Inclusive Approaches to Preventing Violent Conflict.* Washington, DC: World Bank.

WGI (Worldwide Governance Indicators). 2019. Database, World Bank, Washington, DC (accessed October 15, 2019). https://databank.worldbank.org/source/worldwide-governance-indicators.

Windgassen, S., R. Moss-Morris, K. Goldsmith, and T. Chalder. 2018. "The Importance of Cluster Analysis for Enhancing Clinical Practice: An Example from Irritable Bowel Syndrome." *Journal of Mental Health* 27 (2): 94.

World Bank. 2015. *Chad—Priorities for Ending Poverty and Boosting Shared Prosperity: Systematic Country Diagnostic.* Washington, DC: World Bank.

World Bank. 2017. *World Development Report 2017: Governance and the Law.* Washington, DC: World Bank.

WDI (World Development Indicators). 2019. Database. World Bank, Washington, DC (accessed October 15, 2019). https://databank.worldbank.org/source/world-development-indicators.

5. Conclusion—Directions for Action on Fragility and Poverty

This book has painted a stark picture of poverty in fragile and conflict-affected situations (FCS), including its rising prevalence, its impact on multiple dimensions of welfare, and the diversity of country risk profiles that affect its outcomes. The book has shown how, by weakening human capital, fragility and conflict deplete the very resources countries most urgently need to overcome poverty. It has made the case that the global fight to end extreme poverty cannot succeed without delivering solutions for poverty reduction in FCS.

Detailed prescriptions for such solutions lie beyond the scope of this study. But in concluding the book, we highlight four directions for action based on its findings: tackling data deprivation, monitoring markers of fragility to enable prevention and limit adverse welfare impacts, prioritizing and targeting countries and vulnerable groups, and setting context-differentiated, evidence-based policy priorities.

Addressing Data Deprivation

Chapters 1 and 2 documented the wide prevalence of data deprivation concerning poverty and other dimensions of welfare in FCS. In some cases, institutional capacity and resources to design and implement surveys are severely limited. In others, large parts of a country's territory cannot be reached, due to conflict and/or poor infrastructure that hamper the efforts of data collection agencies and threaten their workers' safety. In contexts like the Republic of Yemen, where active conflict is ongoing, no part of the country can currently be accessed safely to conduct large-scale surveys.[1]

Another dimension of data deprivation is the lack of coverage of displaced populations.[2] Developing countries generally do not include nonnationals or refugees in sampling frames and so do not properly capture these groups in national household and labor force surveys; neither do these countries systematically update their frames to reflect internal displacement. Jordan is a recent, notable exception, and other efforts to systematically include displaced populations in national surveys are underway (box 5.1).[3] If surveys are not representative of refugees, internally displaced people, and hosts, then they are not likely to provide the evidence base for policies that support a long-term development response in countries affected by protracted displacement crises.

Counting the Displaced

In countries that have experienced an influx of refugees or internal displacement, the World Bank, in close collaboration with national statistical agencies and other partners, has invested to support the inclusion of displaced populations in national household surveys. Early efforts include innovation in data collection methods and analysis to assess the impact of refugee influxes in Lebanon, Jordan, and Iraq—for example, with the Syrian Refugee and Host Community Survey 2015/16 (World Bank 2016)—and surveys of refugees and migrants (asylum seekers) in Greece and Italy. More recent examples include a survey of refugees and hosts in Bangladesh—Cox's Bazar Panel Survey 2019 (Guglielmi et al. 2019; IPA 2019) and the refugee and host community survey in Ecuador (2019) in the wake of the Venezuelan crises.

Such efforts have also paved the way for more sustainable approaches to filling data gaps on displaced populations. In Africa, the first wave of countries that have added refugee populations to their core poverty survey includes Uganda, Chad, and Niger, with others soon to follow. In Jordan, the household survey of 2017/18 is the first in the country and in the Middle East and North Africa region that is representative of all residents of Jordan, including nonnational populations. Comprehensive surveys covering internally displaced populations were also recently conducted in four countries in Sub-Saharan Africa (Nigeria, Somalia, South Sudan, and Sudan) and in Iraq. The new Joint Data Center for Forced Displacement, established in 2019, is a collaboration between the United Nations High Commissioner for Refugees and the World Bank to promote systematic production of and access to global displacement data.

A third dimension of data deprivation is the lack of data on different markers of fragility at a level of granularity that supports country diagnostics and policy analysis. Over the years, data sets have grown to capture different markers of fragility at the country level.[4] These have proved useful in many applications, as evidenced in the clustering analysis in this book. However, these indicators are seldom available at a regional or subnational level. This impedes more nuanced diagnostics, as conflicts are often focused subnationally, particularly when they first erupt. Without addressing such data gaps, authorities will not be able to effectively monitor factors for fragility and conflict and deploy robust prevention strategies.

Fortunately, this area has recently seen considerable innovation, both in terms of the information collected and how it is obtained. Recent efforts leverage new technologies to measure and monitor an array of important indicators. Much of this innovation has happened in FCS, precisely because the severe field challenges and capacity constraints force practitioners to find creative solutions. The availability of geospatial data, mobile records, and information from social media is now opening doors for new modes of data collection and analytic methods. This may inform and improve population frames and generate an understanding of socioeconomic conditions and welfare at granular levels of spatial disaggregation. Such technologies have also significantly reduced the costs of data collection and the time needed to gather critical data.[5]

Several recent examples illustrate how innovative programs are leveraging technology for applications in development policy relevant to conflict, fragility, and poverty:

- *Tracking returnees, displaced people, or mobile populations:* In Afghanistan, random digit dialing and interactive voice recognition have been used to implement mobile phone surveys to track and monitor outcomes for Afghans returning from decades of displacement abroad. During Mali's recent security crises, to fill an urgent need for policies to support the displaced, a mobile survey collected information about displaced people's location and living conditions. In Somalia, global positioning system trackers were used to understand the migration patterns of nomads, facilitating the inclusion of these populations in surveys.

- *Filling gaps in data on living conditions during conflict:* Given the security situation in the Republic of Yemen, there is little opportunity to conduct traditional household surveys that are representative of the population. However, the need for disaggregated welfare statistics at high frequency is acute, as conditions on the ground are changing rapidly, amid what the United Nations calls the worst humanitarian disaster in the world. Monthly mobile phone surveys are conducted to assess food security and coping mechanisms. These surveys have recently been extended to include additional welfare dimensions relevant to the conflict. The data are playing a critical role in partially addressing acute data gaps for humanitarian and development assistance in the country.

- *Using geospatial data to update population estimates:* In many countries, population census data are outdated, sometimes by decades, due to capacity constraints, political instability, or conflict. And yet, for virtually any policy, having up-to-date knowledge of population distribution is essential. Practitioners rely on population frames for sampling frames to conduct surveys that measure and monitor various aspects of living conditions. High-resolution satellite imagery, microcensuses, and large-scale surveys were used in Afghanistan to develop models that produce grid-level population estimates, a vast improvement in foundational data for a country where the last census was held in 1979. In another novel application, detailed settlement mapping was produced along with population estimates combining high-resolution imagery with geocoded household survey data. The resulting data support a vaccination tracking system and inform broader humanitarian policy and programming (Wardrop et al. 2018).

- *Using cellular trace data to infer welfare and track displaced populations:* The dramatic increase in mobile phone access has led to increased use of mobile surveys. It has also enabled the use of cellular trace data from mobile phone records to infer wealth distribution in countries. Recent work in Rwanda uses anonymized data from the cell phone network to derive wealth distribution in the country, yielding estimates that are comparable to predictions based on the Demographic and Health Surveys (DHS) (Blumenstock, Cadamuro, and On 2015). The same authors have recently applied mobile phone data to understand patterns and motives for migration and location choices. This work holds great promise for framing migration policy.

Monitoring Fragility Markers

According to the Institute for Economics and Peace (2019), the global cost of violence in 2018 was roughly US$14.1 trillion. For comparison, that amount would be sufficient to give every individual on the planet a little over $1,850 for that year. And this does not account for the significant long-term welfare costs, for example, through human capital losses, that are associated with exposure to conflict (chapter 3). The clear lesson is that policies are urgently needed that can help prevent conflict before it starts.

To define and implement such policies, the capacity to monitor markers for fragility and conflict is critical. Decision makers need to determine where conflict threatens to erupt and take preemptive action. Recent advances in data science may again prove valuable. New tools and strategies include detailed open source data from satellite imagery, as well as from social media, combined with techniques like machine learning. These methods hold promise to dramatically improve the monitoring of FCS markers and support the development of early warning systems to guide prevention policies.

Chapter 4 of this book presented a clustering approach to identify countries that are differentiated by distinct markers or fragility profiles. However, the main challenge to effective monitoring is the adequacy and availability of data on important factors associated with fragility at regular periodicity and with sufficient sensitivity to country context.

The existing indicators used as markers of FCS are, for the most part, available only at the national level and could easily mask problematic local situations. Household survey data today afford more regional and subnational disaggregation on living conditions, including poverty, inequality, access to services, labor market outcomes, and safety nets. However, other important data are seldom collected, including indicators that capture local governance or assess political attitudes and grievances, dissatisfaction with government and public services, trust in government, and perceptions of safety and security.

Opportunities exist for ramping up context-specific information on potential local drivers of fragility and conflict. These include but also extend beyond surveys and censuses or novel use of "big data." For example, data generated through evaluating projects and interventions (which can be geographically granular) may contribute powerfully to addressing the need for subnational and local information. Embedding learning systems within operations in FCS contexts or countries identified as vulnerable to fragility can support effective project implementation and also facilitate monitoring of key markers of fragility.

Going beyond monitoring, robust prediction models could help policy makers and their teams design interventions to address the conflict factors found to be most important in specific settings. As with monitoring, however, most prediction models in the literature currently operate at country scale and are far from accurate in their predictions. In addition, they may mask local conflict events that could and should have implications for national-level policy choices. The ideal prediction model, therefore, would be one that can predict conflict both in terms of location (where it is likely to occur) and timing (when it will occur).

Currently, such early warning systems remain embryonic, particularly in terms of predicting the timing of conflict. A recent attempt at testing alternative subnational prediction models (Bazzi et al. 2019) uses 20 years of rich subnational microdata along with granular data on violence. The approach succeeded in predicting conflict locations but was unable to correctly anticipate the timing of new outbreaks of violence. Further work is therefore needed to refine such models and improve their predictive power using additional data from social media, text analysis through newspapers, and more satellite and mobile phone data.

Finally, while monitoring and early warning systems help to identify hot spots and signs of deterioration, designing policies and interventions for mitigation inevitably demands a better understanding of the mechanisms that actually trigger violence. For instance, there is some evidence of climate shocks triggering conflict through direct income losses or indirectly through commodity price shocks. In cases where the channels of impact are clear, as with income loss and conflict, social protection through workfare or cash transfer programs can be particularly effective in protecting households that face negative income shocks, thereby reducing conflict risk. Indeed, analysis in India clearly suggests that the countrywide National Rural Employment Guarantee Act, a workfare program that guarantees 100 days of employment at minimum wage for rural households, has had a significant impact in mitigating the risk of conflict by insulating households from income shocks induced by rainfall patterns (Fetzer 2019). In general, policy research on the causes and underlying mechanisms of conflict remains nascent, as does evidence on what works to mitigate the risks of conflict and why.

Prioritizing and Focusing Policy Action

Diagnostics in this book point to the urgency of focusing on FCS and Sub-Saharan Africa to achieve the Sustainable Development Goal of reducing extreme poverty. Chapter 1 showed that, while Sub-Saharan Africa accounts for the largest share of the extreme poor living in FCS, one in five people in the Middle East and North Africa now live in close proximity to violent conflict, with chronic violence likely to further increase regional poverty.

Nearly half of the economies in Sub-Saharan Africa and the Middle East and North Africa, and more than half of all low-income economies, are classified as FCS. To maximize impact, policy and programming in FCS must be context-differentiated, spatially targeted, and guided by clear strategic priorities. Here, we discuss three potential approaches that countries and international partners may consider in defining priorities and targeting action. One possible lens is the overlap among three factors: long-term conflict, high-intensity conflict, and a large population living in extreme poverty. Arguably, countries in which two or more of these conditions converge are in exceptional need of swift, concerted action to check violence, address humanitarian needs, build and strengthen institutions and the social fabric, and manage generational deficits in human capital and access to services.

Figure 5.1a visualizes the three dimensions and identifies economies in which they overlap. Five economies (Central African Republic, Democratic Republic of Congo, Somalia, South Sudan, and the Republic of Yemen) are currently experiencing two of these three conditions, while in Afghanistan all three of the factors converge. Out of the 37 economies currently in FCS, these six economies are in particular need of assistance from this point of view.

A second approach could be to focus attention in those countries that account for the largest shares of the extreme poor living in FCS. Today, Nigeria and the Democratic Republic of Congo alone are home to 57 percent of all poor people in FCS (figure 5.1b). Thus, with the first Sustainable Development Goal in mind—to end extreme poverty by 2030—focusing on these two countries is vital.

All economies with at least 10 million poor people and/or in high-intensity conflict rank among the bottom quarter of performers on the Human Capital Index (HCI). Based on a human capital lens alone, these economies would logically be among those to focus on. Nigeria has the sixth-lowest HCI score among all countries, while the Democratic Republic of Congo has the twelfth lowest. All five economies with lower HCI results than Nigeria are also in FCS.

FIGURE 5.1   Potential Criteria for Prioritizing and Targeting Policy Action in FCS

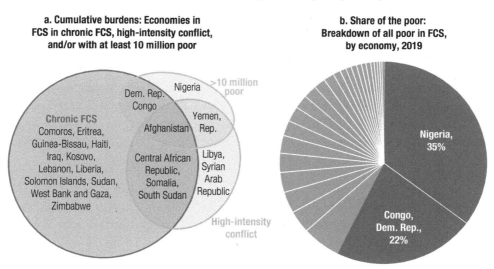

a. Cumulative burdens: Economies in FCS in chronic FCS, high-intensity conflict, and/or with at least 10 million poor

b. Share of the poor: Breakdown of all poor in FCS, by economy, 2019

Note: Poverty numbers are based on 2019 nowcasts from chapter 1.

Questions of targeting apply not just to countries and population groups but also to the hierarchy of needs to be addressed at community and individual levels in FCS. As basic survival needs are tackled, other concerns vital for people's postconflict recovery and well-being must not be neglected. Research on mitigating the long-term impacts of conflict underscores the importance of targeting health and education services to disproportionately vulnerable groups, including women and girls. Conflict exposure among women affects many aspects of their well-being and that of their children, including women's investments in prenatal care and safe delivery. Prioritizing these fundamental interventions can reduce the risk of long-term harms, including among women and children who face compounded vulnerability as refugees or internally displaced persons. Similarly, children's resilience and psychological well-being depend critically on mental health in their parents and/or caregivers. Improving access to mental health services in areas affected by conflict, displacement, or instability is a priority to limit intergenerational transmission of poor mental health outcomes and their severe consequences for welfare.

In settings of ongoing conflict, such as the Republic of Yemen, delivery of all services is challenging. In these contexts, identifying what can be delivered as basic support while doing no harm to exacerbate existing risks is critical. This requires an understanding of potential delivery mechanisms, identifying and working with credible actors and institutions, and being flexible to changing conditions.

The foregoing approaches suggest focusing attention on a set of countries or vulnerable populations that are generally characterized by a long and/or intense exposure to conflict, together with deep-rooted development, governance, and human capital challenges. The methods proposed offer objective criteria for such prioritization.

Privileging Prevention

A different approach is needed to prevent economies from entering FCS in the first place or to act early to mitigate risks and limit exposures. The data-driven clustering exercise presented in the previous chapter is one method by which economies can be distinguished based on a similarity of fragility profiles, but it does not predict future FCS status. As the exercise demonstrates, profiles vary widely and go beyond the more obvious conflict and violence scenarios. The clustering analysis highlights, for instance, distinctive fragility markers linked to a combination of poor governance and abundant natural resources, driving rent seeking by competing interest groups. It also points to the important role in some settings of chronic institutional fragility, lack of voice and participatory processes, and an ineffective or absent state. The exercise identifies an additional subset of economies whose existing fragility may be exacerbated by spillovers from neighboring conflicts, including large-scale population movements. It is possible to define broad-based policy priorities based on this typology (Grävingholt, Ziaja, and Kreibaum 2012) (table 5.1).

TABLE 5.1   **Fragility and Conflict Profiles and Policy Priorities**

Group	Character	Priority goal	Policy focus
Group 1: Low risk (includes small island states with institutional fragility)	Above-average voice and accountability, political stability and absence of violence, and government effectiveness	Strengthen economic fundamentals and institutional capacity in small states	Small island states: Build state capacity for economic management; strengthen connectivity to larger economic zones; international support to manage climate and disaster risks
Group 2: Crime and violence risk	Limited voice and accountability, high homicides per 100,000 people	Reduce crime and violence; address perceptions of unfairness and injustice	Strengthen state capacity to deliver law, order, and justice; support state legitimacy; support regional and global initiatives on criminal networks
Group 3: Periodic monitoring	No salient characteristic	Monitor risks	Where risks are elevated, country-level analysis should direct the nature of support
Group 4: Regional spillover and fragility risks	High refugee population in relation to hosts	Address economic fragility exacerbated by political, security, and economic spillovers from neighboring countries	Strengthen state capacity for service delivery; better management of macro risks, including expanding scope of existing disaster and shocks facilities at WB and IMF to manage shocks linked to displacement; burden-sharing mechanisms (regional and global)
Group 5: Rent-seeking and resource-conflict risk	Natural resources, poor governance, ethnic fractionalization	Build transparency and accountability in the management of resource rents	Fiscal management of resource wealth; fiscal federalism; economic diversification; instruments for broad-based benefits and service delivery (including spatially); coordinated action on illicit flows, tax information sharing; policies that help reduce elite capture
Group 6: Conflict	High battle deaths, poor governance, political instability and violence, ethnic fractionalization	Establish basic security and rule of law; deliver quick wins to citizens; rebuild trust	Broad-based international engagement; peacekeeping and peacebuilding; catalyzing action on potential conflict financing (AML and CFT, "conflict diamonds"); UN sanctions

Note: AML = anti-money-laundering; CFT = countering financing of terrorism; IMF = International Monetary Fund; UN = United Nations; WB = World Bank.

Such wide-ranging diversity in fragility markers necessitates a finely differentiated approach to policy and program delivery. To make this possible, monitoring must be timely and subnational, and continuous learning must be built in as a core component of programs implemented across varied FCS contexts.

Fighting Poverty on the Front Lines

Global poverty goals will not be reached without dramatic and sustained poverty reduction in FCS economies, where the majority of the world's poor will live as of late 2020. Delay or ineffective measures now will raise the cost of action later and leave intractable poverty in FCS as a divisive legacy for future generations.

Opportunities exist now to improve outcomes among poor people in FCS by

- Tackling data deprivation
- Improving monitoring and conflict prediction
- Prioritizing and targeting resources to the places most in need
- Setting context-differentiated, evidence-based policy priorities.

These four points do not define a comprehensive plan for breaking cycles of poverty and conflict. But advances in these four domains will lay foundations on which subsequent policy and programming initiatives can build. Without progress in these cornerstone areas, it will be difficult to advance the many other policies that will be required to address specific welfare needs and progressively bring down poverty in FCS.

As this book's analysis of country fragility profiles showed, heterogeneous contexts among FCS mean that repairing fragility and addressing extreme poverty in these settings will require a nuanced, context-informed, and evidence-based approach. The strategy will need broad buy-in from global partners and will have to anchor positive incentives at all levels, from diplomacy to frontline implementation. Resources must be committed to continuous learning and evidence generation, as well as early action.

The success or failure of these efforts will matter in the first place to poor people in FCS. For many, indeed, how well these policies work will determine their chances of survival. That the hopes and often the lives of millions of the world's most vulnerable people hang in the balance is reason enough to act. But the benefits of reducing poverty and expanding opportunity in FCS will extend far beyond the populations directly concerned, and beyond the boundaries of FCS.

Global events offer daily confirmation that poverty reduction and conflict resolution or their absence in FCS have inescapable geopolitical significance. The widening repercussions of violence and instability in Afghanistan, Syria, Ukraine, the Republic of Yemen, and other settings show that the destinies of FCS will affect the rest of the world. Economies of FCS stand on the front lines of the struggle to end extreme poverty. But the outcome of that struggle will shape the human future everywhere.

Notes

1. Conflict also leads to the loss of data infrastructure or its steady erosion, often destroying the records of previous painstaking data collection work. During the civil war in the Central African Republic, for instance, much of the country's data infrastructure (buildings, books, maps, servers, and computers) was lost to looting.
2. Low- and middle-income countries seldom have a data infrastructure in place that can flexibly adapt to large-scale population movements. Indeed, foundational administrative data and population censuses are often out of date, incomplete, or missing altogether. Consequently, displaced populations are typically left out of regular statistical data collection.

3. The latest round of the Jordanian national household income and expenditure survey, in 2018, includes an explicit stratum for non-Jordanians (World Bank 2018).

4. See, for example, Celiku and Kraay (2017) and appendix C, which lists data sets that are typically used to assess fragility and conflict.

5. See more detailed examples and descriptions in Hoogeveen and Pape (2020).

References

Bazzi, S., R. A. Blair, C. Blattman, O. Dube, M. Gudgeon, and R. M. Peck. 2019. "The Promise and Pitfalls of Conflict Prediction: Evidence from Colombia and Indonesia." Working paper 25980, National Bureau of Economic Research, Cambridge, MA.

Blumenstock, J. E., G. Cadamuro, and R. On. 2015. "Predicting Poverty and Wealth from Mobile Phone Metadata." *Science* 350: 1073–1076.

Celiku, B., and A. Kraay. 2017. "Predicting Conflict." Policy Research Working Paper 8075, World Bank, Washington, DC.

Fetzer, T. 2019. "Can Workfare Programs Moderate Conflict? Evidence from India." *Journal of the European Economic Association*. Preprint. https://www.eeassoc.org/doc/paper/20191008_132542 _FETZER_NREGA.PDF.

Grävingholt, Jörn, Sebastian Ziaja, and Merle Kreibaum. 2012. "State Fragility: Towards a Multi-Dimensional Empirical Typology." DIE discussion paper 3/2012, SSRN, Rochester, NY. https:// ssrn.com/abstract=2279407.

Guglielmi, S., J. Muz, K. Mitu, M. Ala Uddin, N. Jones, S. Baird, and E. Presler-Marshall. 2019. *The Lives They Lead: Exploring the Capabilities of Bangladeshi and Rohingya Adolescents in Cox's Bazar, Bangladesh*. Policy brief, London: Gender and Adolescence: Global Evidence.

Hoogeveen, J. G., and U. Pape. 2020. *Data Collection in Fragile States: Innovations from Africa and Beyond*. Washington, DC: World Bank Group.

Institute for Economics and Peace. 2019. *Global Peace Index 2019: Measuring Peace in a Complex World*. Sydney. http://visionofhumanity.org/app/uploads/2019/07/GPI-2019web.pdf.

IPA (Innovations for Poverty Action). 2019. "The Impact of Large-Scale Forced Displacement on Rohingya Refugees and Host Communities in Cox's Bazar, Bangladesh." Project description, IPA, New Haven, CT. (accessed January 12, 2020). https://www.poverty-action.org/study /impact-large-scale-forced-displacement-rohingya-refugees-and-host-communities-cox's -bazar#_ftnref1.

Wardrop, N. A., W. C. Jochem, T. J. Bird, H. R. Chamberlain, D. Clarke, D. Kerr, et al. 2018. "Spatially Disaggregated Population Estimates in the Absence of National Population and Housing Census Data." *Proceedings of the National Academy of Sciences* 115 (14): 3529–37.

World Bank. 2016. *Survey of Syrian Refugees and Host Communities, 2015–2016*. Washington, DC: World Bank. (accessed January 12, 2020). https://microdata.worldbank.org/index.php/ catalog/3471.

World Bank. 2018. *Jordan Household Expenditure and Income Survey 2017–18: Completion Note*. Washington, DC: World Bank.

Appendix A: Computing Proximity to Conflict

Data Processing

In order to calculate the number of people living in close proximity to conflict, data from the Uppsala Conflict Data Program (UCDP) are used. All georeferenced conflict events with 25 or more battle-related deaths were selected. These are denoted major conflict events. Only events where at least the second-order administrative division of the location of the event is known are kept (denoted precision level 1, 2, or 3 in the UCDP data). When the exact location is not known, UCDP typically uses the centroid to present the event.

Once the major conflict events were selected, 60-kilometer buffers were generated around each of the events. With the buffers generated, zonal statistics geoprocessing was conducted on the 2012 LandScan population raster data in order to estimate the total population residing in each buffer for all countries. With the summed population in close proximity to conflict for all countries, the share of each country's population that lives in close proximity to conflict can be calculated. Since the LandScan population raster data were available only for 2012, the analysis proxies the global population distribution from 2007 to 2017, with the global population distribution from 2012. See figure A.1.

Caveats and Limitations

- The UCDP dataset does not make conflict events for the Syrian Arab Republic public, as the data are not of the same standard nor are they available for all years. Nevertheless, the Syrian data were requested from UCDP, which provided the data. The data were merged with the rest of the conflict data and included in the analysis, with the exception of the years 2012 to 2014 (see next bullet).
- In the case of the Syrian Arab Republic, UCDP does not have data for the years 2012, 2013, and 2014. For those years, the analysis assumes that 100 percent of the population was in close proximity to conflict. This is only slightly higher than the years following 2014, which registered 95, 91, and 85 percent of the population as being in close proximity to conflict.
- This exercise is not constrained by country borders; hence, it counts population within the buffers regardless of country boundaries.

FIGURE A.1 **One in Five People in the Middle East and North Africa Lives in Close Proximity to Conflict**

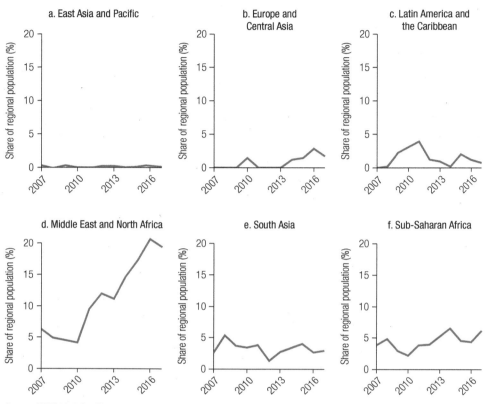

Sources: UCDP 2019; LandScan 2012.

Note: Individuals are considered to live in close proximity to conflict if they are within 60 kilometers of a major conflict event, defined as 25 or more battle-related deaths in the year in question.

- The 60-kilometer buffer is a Euclidean distance from the conflict event rather than distance by roads.
- This method is very sensitive to conflict events that occur in heavily populated areas. One major conflict event or act of terror occurring in the center of a major city could significantly increase the share of the population that lives in close proximity to conflict in that country. One example of this was the 2016 Nice truck attack, which caused portions of France and 100 percent of Monaco to be in close proximity to conflict in 2016.

References

LandScan. 2012. High-Resolution Global Population Data Set. Oak Ridge National Laboratory, Oak Ridge, TN (accessed October 15, 2019), https://landscan.ornl.gov.

UCDP (Uppsala Conflict Data Program). 2019. *UCDP Conflict Encyclopedia.* Uppsala, Sweden: Department of Peace and Conflict Research, Uppsala University (accessed October 15, 2019), https://www.ucdp.uu.se.

Appendix B: Methods to Address Poverty Data Deprivation

Several strategies are explored in this book to tackle and work around data shortages concerning poverty in fragile and conflict-affected situations (FCS).

Economies with No International Poverty Estimates

The World Bank's international poverty numbers currently do not have any explicit poverty rates for economies that lack data altogether. Nevertheless, these economies implicitly feature in the global poverty counts by being assigned the population weighted average poverty rate of the region the economy belongs to. If economies in FCS on average are poorer than the region as a whole, then this method would underestimate poverty in economies in FCS. To account for this issue, in this book, gross domestic product (GDP) per capita in purchasing power terms is used to predict poverty rates for economies without data. Specifically, economies that have data both on international poverty and GDP per capita are used to generate a relationship between the two, such that poverty rates can subsequently be estimated based on GDP per capita alone.

It is plausible that this relationship differs for economies in FCS and economies not in FCS. A different relationship could emerge if economies in FCS are worse at converting GDP per capita into consumption and thereby poverty reduction. This might be the case if economies in FCS are more unequal, or if a fraction of the GDP in economies in FCS, due to corruption, military spending, or for another reason, does not trickle down to the general population.

Figure B.1a shows the relationship between GDP per capita and poverty for economies in FCS and other economies using the backcasted FCS status from 2000 to 2019. The relationship is nearly identical across the two country groups, and the differences are not statistically significant at the 5 percent level, suggesting that the concerns described in the preceding paragraph are not relevant. This finding is robust to using data from the Harmonized Lists of Fragile Situations (the historical FCS classification) and data from the Armed Conflict Location and Event Data Project (ACLED) or the Uppsala Conflict Data Program (UCDP) to define whether economies are in FCS (if they have at least 1 conflict death per 100,000 people). Based on this relationship, poverty can be estimated based on GDP per capita. In particular, a fractional logit regression is used to predict US$1.90 poverty rates given a level of GDP per capita in 2011 US$ purchasing power parity (PPP), with the following formula:

$$poverty\ rate = \frac{exp(11.359 - 3.560 * log_{10}(GDP/capita))}{1 + exp(11.359 - 3.560 * log_{10}(GDP/capita))}$$

Some economies lack data on GDP per capita as well, either because of absent national accounts, or because they lack the consumer prices and PPPs that are necessary to express GDP in the same unit across countries and across time. In these cases, satellite imagery of an economy's nightlights is used to get an estimate of GDP per capita. Satellite imagery has been shown to be highly predictive of GDP per capita in past analyses (Bruederle and Hodler 2018; Henderson, Vernon, and Weil 2012; Pinkovskiy and Sala-i-Martin 2016). As nightlights are available across the world, this can be used to infer poverty rates even for economies without GDP data. GDP per capita in 2011 US dollar PPP is predicted from a second-order polynomial of the log of area lit per capita (figure B.1b).[1] With these two strategies, using GDP per capita and nightlights, it is possible to proxy poverty rates for economies in FCS (and all other economies) without data.[2]

FIGURE B.1 **Relationship between Poverty Rates, GDP per Capita, and Nighttime Lights**

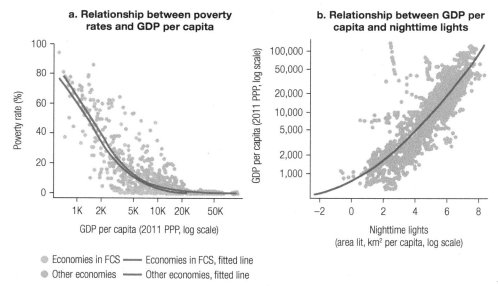

a. Relationship between poverty rates and GDP per capita

b. Relationship between GDP per capita and nighttime lights

Economies in FCS ——— Economies in FCS, fitted line
Other economies ——— Other economies, fitted line

Sources: PovcalNet (online analysis tool), World Bank, Washington, DC, http://iresearch.worldbank.org/PovcalNet/; WDI (NY.GDP. PCAP.PP.KD); VIIRS, image and data processing by the National Oceanic and Atmospheric Administration's National Geophysical Data Center.

Note: FCS status is defined by applying the 2020 criteria retrospectively. See box 1.3, chapter 1, for details. The fitted line is based on a fractional logistic regression. FCS = fragile and conflict-affected situations; GDP = gross domestic product; km² = square kilometers; PPP = purchasing power parity.

Economies with No Recent Poverty Estimates

For economies in FCS where some poverty data exist, but they are outdated, the World Bank generally assumes that the growth in GDP per capita (or household final consumption expenditure) registered since the economy's last reliable survey with an international poverty estimate is fully passed through to the consumption vector from that survey. In general, this assumption works fairly well for economies that are not in FCS. Using household surveys conducted over the past 20 years reveals that, on average, 96 percent of growth in GDP per capita is passed through to the income or consumption observed in household surveys. Statistically, one cannot rule out that all growth in GDP per capita is passed through to the consumption vector for economies not in FCS (figure B.2).

Although one could apply this relationship to economies in FCS as well, it is plausible that growth in GDP per capita may not be fully passed through to consumption for these economies. Data are more scant, but for the 77 cases of economies that were in FCS between two surveys, again using the backcasted list, the best guess is that only 42 percent of growth is passed through to consumption, and a pass-through rate of

FIGURE B.2 Share of Growth in GDP per Capita Passed through to the Consumption Vector

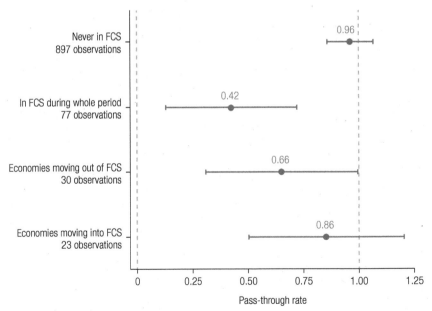

Sources: PovcalNet (online analysis tool), World Bank, Washington, DC, http://iresearch.worldbank.org/PovcalNet/; WDI (NY.GDP.PCAP.PP.KD).

Note: The figure shows how much a 1 percent growth in GDP per capita is expected to increase growth in mean consumption per capita for different groups of economies. The bars indicate 95th confidence bands. FCS are defined using the backcasted list (see box 1.3, chapter 1, for details). FCS = fragile and conflict-affected situations.

100 percent is statistically implausible. For 30 cases of economies that entered FCS status between two surveys, the pass-through rate is 66 percent. For 23 economies that escaped FCS status, the pass-through rate is 86 percent, which in this case does not represent a statistically significant difference from 100 percent (figure B.2).

The small number of cases of economies escaping or entering FCS makes it difficult to narrow exactly *how much* growth in GDP per capita matters, particularly given that in some of these cases the economies were in FCS during most of the period considered, while in others perhaps only for a year. To leverage the full power of the data, annualized growth in the survey mean is regressed on annualized growth in GDP per capita together with an interaction of annualized growth in GDP per capita and the share of time spent as FCS:

$$growth_{survey\ mean} = \underset{(0.052)}{0.964} * growth_{GDP/capita} - \underset{(0.137)}{0.530} * growth_{GDP/capita} * share\ as\ FCS$$

For economies never in FCS, 96 percent of GDP growth is passed through to welfare, while for economies in FCS during the entire period, 43 percent $(0.964 - 0.530)$ is passed through. If the economy spent a quarter of the time in FCS between two periods, then 83 percent $(0.964 - 0.25*0.530)$ is passed through. In other words, for every year an economy is in FCS, approximately half of the growth is passed through, while for every year not in FCS, all growth is passed through. We use this relation to adjust current poverty extrapolations. For economies in FCS where GDP per capita plunged, which often happens in high-intensity conflict, this implies that poverty rates will be adjusted *downward*, since there is only evidence for half of this plunge in GDP per capita transferring to household consumption. Conversely, for economies in FCS that experience growth in GDP per capita, poverty rates will be adjusted upward.[3]

In general, this means that, when an economy experiences conflict, violence, or fragility, GDP per capita moves more than does welfare, or, in other words, that GDP per capita tends to exhibit larger swings than changes in welfare. A likely reason for this is the destruction and rebuilding of infrastructure that often occur during conflict, as this tends to cause large changes in some of the components of GDP (Collier et al. 2003). Although this certainly matters for household welfare, it is likely that GDP moves more rapidly. In conflict situations, governments may also increase military spending, which—all else equal—adds to GDP but not to household consumption (Gupta et al. 2004).[4]

An alternative method often applied to obtain contemporary poverty estimates for economies with outdated data is to use growth elasticities of poverty. This approach does not rely on the assumption implicit in the preceding paragraphs—that growth accrues equally to everyone. Growth elasticities of poverty reveal the percentage change in poverty rates that results from a 1 percent growth in GDP per capita. Such elasticities are intuitive, since they directly reflect how well growth in GDP per capita is converted

Using Elasticities to Nowcast and Forecast Poverty

Using growth in GDP per capita to move up the entire distribution of welfare to the year for which poverty should be expressed relies on two important assumptions. The first is that growth in GDP per capita is fully passed through to the welfare vector. As discussed, this assumption can be adjusted rather straightforwardly. The second assumption is that there is no change in the distribution of welfare between the year of the survey and the year for which poverty should be expressed. This means that it is assumed that inequality remains unchanged.

An alternative, more direct way of nowcasting poverty rates that bypasses this assumption is to use growth elasticities of poverty. Growth elasticities of poverty reveal the percentage change in poverty rates as a result of a 1 percent growth in GDP per capita. Although such elasticities are intuitive, because they directly reflect how well growth in GDP per capita is converted into poverty reduction, they come with some measurement challenges. Most importantly, elasticities are mechanically dependent on the initial poverty level such that one can expect elasticities to improve as economies become wealthier (Beegle et al. 2016). This makes it problematic to use a historical elasticity for an economy and to keep the value fixed to project forward, if this economy in the meanwhile has lowered its poverty rate.

FIGURE BB.1.1   Growth Elasticities of Poverty as a Function of Initial Poverty Rate

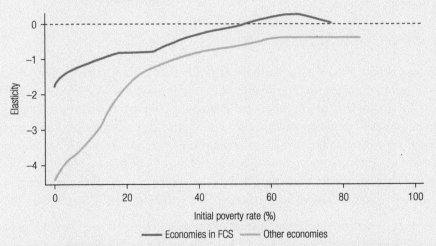

Sources: PovcalNet (online analysis tool), World Bank, Washington, DC, http://iresearch.worldbank.org/PovcalNet/; WDI (NY.GDP.PCAP.PP.KD).

Note: The figure shows how much 1 percent growth in GDP per capita is expected to change poverty as a function of FCS status and initial poverty level. The backcasted FCS list is used to define FCS status (see box 1.3, chapter 1, for details). An elasticity of, for example, 2, means that 1 percent growth in GDP per capita is associated with a 2 percent decline in the poverty rate. The figure is a result of a weighted regression of growth in poverty on growth in GDP per capita. The coefficient from this regression is the elasticity. Elasticities are computed sequentially for all initial poverty levels, giving larger weights to observations close to the initial poverty rate in question. The weight used for estimating the elasticity at the initial poverty rate of x is max(20-abs(poverty rate-x)).

(Box continues on the following page.)

Using Elasticities to Nowcast and Forecast Poverty *(continued)*

This can be accounted for by making elasticities a function of initial poverty rates. With this approach, calculating elasticities for economies in FCS and economies not in FCS reveals that economies in FCS are systematically worse at converting growth in GDP into poverty reduction (figure BB.1.1). For example, for economies with poverty rates around 20 percent, a 1 percent growth in GDP is associated with a 2 percent decline in poverty for economies not in FCS, but only a 1 percent decline in poverty for economies in FCS. This is consistent with the finding that pass-through rates vary by countries' FCS status.

into poverty reduction. They come with some measurement challenges, as outlined in box B.1, but they too suggest that economies in FCS are not as effective at converting GDP per capita growth into poverty reduction as are economies not in FCS.

Both of these methods to generate poverty estimates for economies with outdated data naturally do not address the main issue, which is that the data at hand are outdated. The first-best solution to this problem is to get newer data. Nonetheless, the methods do improve poverty extrapolations in these situations by leveraging empirical relationships observed in the past.

Poverty among Displaced People

Displaced people living in camps are not sampled in household surveys. With the number of displaced people on the rise and the share of people in extreme poverty falling, this is increasingly a problem for estimates of global poverty (World Bank 2018). Current global poverty counts implicitly assume that displaced people living in camps have the same distribution of welfare as the rest of the country they reside in, which is likely to underestimate poverty.[5] Displaced people are likely to have higher poverty rates since they face weak labor demand, may have been subject to psychological distress, and too often lack access to basic infrastructure services (Beegle and Christiansen 2019).

To circumvent this problem, a small number of country-level studies are leveraged as guideposts to get a sense of what poverty is like for displaced populations. Studies on the poverty of IDPs, refugees, or refugee-like populations have been conducted on three continents, in Iraq, Peru, Somalia, South Sudan, and Uganda. Using these five countries as benchmarks reveals that displaced populations in general have 10–30 percent lower consumption levels than nondisplaced populations living in proximity (table B.1).

Inequality within displaced populations, relative to that among the nondisplaced, varies across the contexts studied: much lower in Peru and much higher in Uganda,

TABLE B.1   **Consumption and Inequality among Displaced People, Five Countries**

Country	Displaced population	Mean relative to nondisplaced population	Gini relative to nondisplaced population
Iraq	IDPs	0.79	1.05
Peru	Venezuelans in refugee-like situations	0.76	0.63
Somalia	IDPs	0.90	1.03
South Sudan	IDPs	0.91	0.86
Uganda	Refugees	0.64	1.34

Sources: Sharma and Wai-Poi 2019; Pape and Parisotto 2019; Pape and Wollburg 2019; Uganda Refugee and Host Communities 2018 Household Survey (results presented in World Bank 2019); staff calculations.
Note: IDPs = internally displaced persons.

for example. On average, however, the displaced and nondisplaced show similar levels of inequality, suggesting that displaced people have roughly the same distribution of welfare as their nondisplaced neighbors, but scaled down by a fixed proportion.

These patterns can be used to estimate the level and distribution of consumption in other situations of displacement. If displaced populations in camps generally have the same distribution of consumption as neighboring nondisplaced people, but scaled down by about 25 percent, then poverty can be modeled among displaced populations in camps. Figure B.3 shows the results of such an exercise for Jordan in 2015.

FIGURE B.3   **Estimating Welfare for Displaced People, Jordan, 2015**

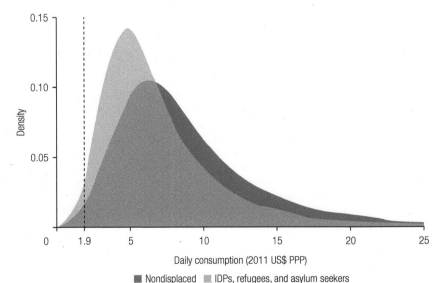

Source: PovcalNet (online analysis tool), World Bank, Washington, DC, http://iresearch.worldbank.org/PovcalNet/.
Note: The figure shows the estimated welfare distribution in Jordan for 2015 and the imputed welfare distribution for displaced people. IDP = internally displaced person; PPP = purchasing power parity.

Displaced people that move into new housing or with nondisplaced relatives are often captured in household surveys. Because the share of displaced people living in camps versus in other housing is not known across countries and years, and to be conservative about progress in global poverty, the rescaling of welfare discussed in the preceding paragraphs is applied to all displaced people.[6] This could imply that the method used here overestimates poverty among displaced people. Provided that welfare among displaced people in camps is lower than welfare among displaced people living outside of camps, this overestimation of poverty would be moderated.

Needless to say, displaced populations and their situations vary widely. Asylum seekers in Norway face very different challenges than do IDPs in Eritrea, for example. However, the assumption that displaced people have the same welfare distribution as their nondisplaced neighbors, but consistently scaled down, is likely more conservative, and perhaps more accurate, than the current implicit assumptions behind global poverty numbers. Hence, while awaiting empirical data, such an assumption can help provide a more accurate picture of poverty in situations of conflict, albeit still an approximation.

Notes

1. Rather than using nighttime lights to predict GDP per capita, and through that, poverty rates, nighttime lights could be used to predict poverty rates directly. Here the former approach is used such that growth rates in GDP per capita can be used to forecast poverty for all economies.

2. Two economies, Channel Islands and Sint Maarten (Dutch part), do not have international poverty data, data on GDP per capita in 2011 PPP, or data on nighttime lights. These two economies are assigned the population-weighted average poverty rate of high-income economies. Since these two economies have a combined population of less than a quarter of a million, this has little impact on global or regional poverty counts.

3. The finding that GDP per capita moves more than average consumption for economies in conflict, fragility, and violence, at face value, seems inconsistent with the finding of the previous subsection; that economies in FCS have the same relationship between GDP per capita and poverty rates as economies not in FCS. If two economies, one in FCS and one not in FCS, have the same GDP per capita, then the finding from the previous subsection would predict that they have the same poverty rate. Suppose now that these two economies grow at the same rate over the next 10 years. The finding in this subsection would suggest that mean consumption in the economy in FCS will be lower after these 10 years, and hence poverty higher. However, as the two economies still have the same GDP per capita, the finding of the last subsection would suggest they have the same poverty rate. How can this happen? One possibility is that with more data points, and hence more statistical power, differences in the relationship between GDP per capita and poverty rates between economies in FCS and those not in FCS would be detected in the previous subsection. Another reconciling factor is that growth in GDP per capita in economies in conflict is quite low on average. If growth in economies in FCS on average is zero, then the inconsistency vanishes. The inconsistency is also diminished by the fact that economies enter and exit FCS status. To use the example from before, suppose that after the 10 years the economies swap FCS status. Then the inconsistency will run in the other direction.

4. An alternative to using growth in GDP per capita to determine pass-through rates and generate extrapolated estimates of poverty is to use growth in household final consumption expenditure (HFCE) per capita, which is the subcomponent of GDP per capita most related to consumption or income as observed in household surveys. A challenge with using HFCE per capita is that it is not available for all economies, particularly not forecasted values of HFCE per capita, which are necessary for projecting poverty to 2030. To avoid dealing with two different models, and generally to simplify matters, this analysis focuses on GDP per capita. In addition, some evidence suggests that using GDP per capita is as precise in nowcasting poverty as using HFCE per capita (Castaneda Aguilar et al. 2019).

5. For internally displaced persons (IDPs), the situation is a bit more complicated. If the census sampling frame was created before the displacement of IDPs, then the IDPs are included in the sampling weights of the area they used to reside in. In these cases, they are not assigned the same welfare as the rest of the country, but the same welfare as the region they resided in. If this region is poorer than the country as a whole, which is the case if poverty is positively associated with conflict within countries, then the underestimation is less severe. To the extent that IDPs are poorer than average within the region where they lived before their displacement, an underestimation still occurs.

6. Some indicative numbers of the share of displaced people living in camps can be found in World Bank (2017).

References

Beegle, Kathleen, and Luc Christiaensen. 2019. *Accelerating Poverty Reduction in Africa*. Washington, DC: World Bank.

Beegle, Kathleen, Luc Christiaensen, Andrew Dabalen, and Isis Gaddis 2016. *Poverty in a Rising Africa*. Washington, DC: World Bank.

Bruederle, Anna, and Roland Hodler. 2018. "Nighttime Lights as a Proxy for Human Development at the Local Level." *PLoS One* 13 (9). https://doi.org/10.1371/journal.pone.0202231.

Castaneda Aguilar, R. Andres, Daniel Gerszon Mahler, and David Newhouse. 2019. "Nowcasting Global Poverty." Paper presented at the Special IARIW-World Bank Conference "New Approaches to Defining and Measuring Poverty in a Growing World," Washington, DC, November 7–8, 2019.

Collier, Paul, V.L. Elliott, Håvard Hegre, Anke Hoeffler, Marta Reynal-Querol, and Nicholas Sambanis. 2003. *Breaking the Conflict Trap: Civil War and Development Policy*. Policy Research Report. Washington, DC: World Bank and Oxford University Press.

Gupta, Sanjeev, Benedict Clements, Rina Bhattacharya, and Shamit Chakravarti. 2004. "Fiscal Consequences of Armed Conflict and Terrorism in Low- and Middle-Income Countries." *European Journal of Political Economy* 20(2): 403–21.

Henderson, J., Adam Storeygard Vernon, and David N. Weil. 2012. "Measuring Economic Growth from Outer Space." *American Economic Review* 102 (2): 994–1028.

Pape, Utz Johann, and Luca Parisotto. 2019. "Estimating Poverty in a Fragile Context—The High Frequency Survey in South Sudan." Policy Research Working Paper 8722, World Bank, Washington, DC.

Pape, Utz Johann, and Philip Randolph Wollburg. 2019. "Estimation of Poverty in Somalia Using Innovative Methodologies." Policy Research Working Paper 8735, World Bank, Washington, DC.

Pinkovskiy, Maxim, and Xavier Sala-i-Martin. 2016. "Lights, Camera . . . Income! Illuminating the National Accounts-Household Surveys Debate." *Quarterly Journal of Economics* 131 (2): 579–631.

Sharma, Dhiraj, and Matthew Grant Wai-Poi. 2019. *Arrested Development: Conflict Displacement and Welfare in Iraq*. Washington, DC: World Bank Group.

WDI (World Development Indicators). 2017. Database. "Total Natural Resources Rents (% of GDP)." Washington, DC: World Bank. https://datacatalog.worldbank.org/dataset/world -development-indicators.

World Bank. 2017. *Forcibly Displaced: Toward a Development Approach Supporting Refugees, the Internally Displaced, and Their Hosts.* Washington, DC: World Bank.

World Bank. 2018. *Poverty and Shared Prosperity 2018: Piecing Together the Poverty Puzzle.* Washington, DC: World Bank.

World Bank. 2019. *Informing the Refugee Policy Response in Uganda: Results from the Uganda Refugee and Host Communities 2018 Household Survey.* Washington, DC: World Bank.

Appendix C: Classification Tree of FCS for Fiscal Year 2020

FIGURE C.1 **Classification Tree for Assigning Economies to the World Bank List of Fragile and Conflict-Affected Situations, Fiscal Year 2020**

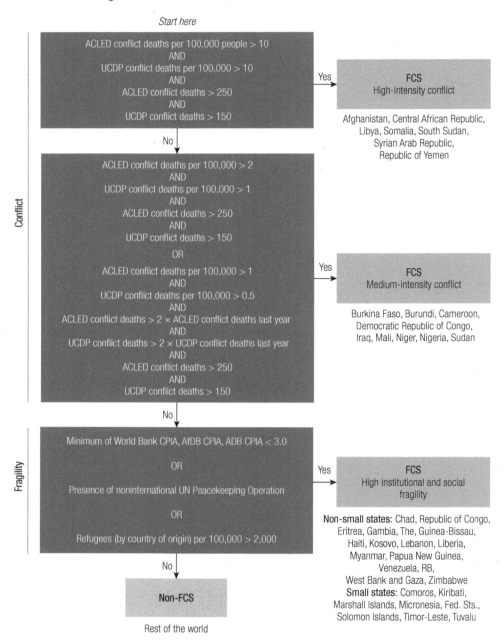

Source: Harmonized List of Fragile Situations, https://www.worldbank.org/en/topic/fragilityconflictviolence/brief/harmonized-list-of-fragile-situations.

Note: ACLED refers to data from the Armed Conflict Location and Event Data Project, https://www.acleddata.com. UCDP refers to data from the Uppsala Conflict Data Program, https://ucdp.uu.se. CPIA refers to Country Policy and Institutional Assessment scores. AfDB refers to the African Development Bank. ADB refers to the Asian Development Bank.

Appendix D: Data Sources for Cluster Analysis

Worldwide Governance Indicators

The Worldwide Governance Indicators (WGI) are aggregate measures of governance built on other data. They cover roughly 200 countries since 1996. The indicators include six dimensions:[1]

- *Voice and accountability* measures the extent to which a country's citizens are able to participate in selecting their government and to enjoy freedom of expression, freedom of association, and a free media.
- *Political stability and absence of violence* measures perceptions of the likelihood of political instability and/or politically motivated violence, including terrorism.
- *Government effectiveness* captures perceptions of the quality of civil service and the degree of its independence from political pressures, the quality of policy formulation and implementation, and the credibility of the government's commitment to such policies.
- *Regulatory quality* captures perceptions of the ability of the government to formulate and implement sound policies and regulations that permit and promote private sector development.
- *Rule of law* captures perceptions of the extent to which agents have confidence in and abide by the rules of society, and in particular the quality of contract enforcement, property rights, the police, and the courts, as well as the likelihood of crime and violence.
- *Control of corruption* captures perceptions of the extent to which public power is exercised for private gain, including both petty and grand forms of corruption, as well as "capture" of the state by elites and private interests.

For a detailed discussion on how the underlying data are made comparable and then put together into the six individual components, readers can refer to Kaufman, Kray, and Mastruzzi (2011).[2]

The latest WGI data available as of this writing—2018—are used in the clustering exercise.

Battle Death Data

Information on battle deaths comes from two primary sources that complement each other. The main data source is the Armed Conflict Location and Event Data Project (ACLED), a disaggregated data collection, analysis, and crisis mapping project. It collects details about fatalities of all reported political violence and protest events across the globe, except for most high-income countries.

An average of the number of fatalities over the country's population for the previous five years is taken. If a country is still missing information, we assign a value of 0. Finally, the values are standardized to mean 0 and standard deviation 1.

Since the data is not collected for Europe, North America, and Latin America, it is possible to complement the information from ACLED with data from the Uppsala Conflict Data Program (UCDP). However the information contained is somewhat different. Qualitatively, the clusters obtained by replacing the missing ACLED data with UCDP data do not differ considerably.[3] The UCDP data comes from Uppsala University, and has been collected for almost 40 years. It includes data on organized violence and armed conflicts. Annual updates have been published every year since 1993 in the *Journal of Peace Research*.

Data on Refugees

Data on refugees come from United Nations High Commissioner for Refugees (UNHCR).[4] Refugees include individuals recognized under the following conventions, statutes, and conditions:[5]

- 1951 Convention Relating to the Status of Refugees and its 1967 Protocol
- The 1969 OAU Convention Governing the Specific Aspects of Refugee Problems in Africa
- UNHCR Statute
- Individuals granted complementary forms of protection
- Those enjoying temporary protection

For most countries, the data come from the government. In nonindustrialized countries, the local government is assisted in the collection of data, along with refugee registration, by UNHCR. For any given country, if information on refugees is missing for a particular year, the information is completed from the previous year. Then an average of the number of refugees over the country's population for the previous five years is taken. Finally, the values are standardized to mean 0 and standard deviation 1.

Data on Natural Resources

Total natural resources as a percentage of gross domestic product (GDP) comes from the World Bank's World Development Indicators (WDI 2017). The indicator is the sum of oil rents, natural gas rents, coal rents, mineral rents, and forest rents over total GDP. The full methodology on how the indicator is obtained can be found in Lange, Wodon, and Carey (2018).

Data on Homicides

Data on homicides comes from the UN Office on Drugs and Crime (UNODC) International Homicide Database. The data are reported as the number of homicides per 100,000 people.[6] Homicides are defined by the International Classification of Crime for Statistical Purposes as the "unlawful death inflicted upon a person with the intent to cause death or serious injury" (UNODC 2019, 7). Every death that fits the defined criteria is classified as an intentional homicide.

If a country does not have information on homicide rates for a given year, the information is completed from the previous year. Then an average of the homicide rates per 100,000 people for the previous five years is taken. Finally, the values are standardized to mean 0 and standard deviation 1.

Data on Ethnic Fractionalization

The data on ethnic fractionalization comes from Alesina et al. (2003). The level of ethnic fractionalization reflects the probability that two randomly selected individuals from a population belonged to different ethnic groups. The data is available only for the year 2003. We assume that this information is unlikely to have changed by a considerable amount since then. For specific countries, where available, information was filled in from different data sources.[7] Finally, the values are standardized to mean 0 and standard deviation 1.

Notes

1. The indicators are collected annually, and the latest available are used for every country. The latest year for which they are available is 2018. For more details, see Kaufman, Kraay, and Mastruzzi (2011).
2. The latest data and information can be found at https://info.worldbank.org/governance/wgi/.
3. The latest data and information on UCDP can be found on the organization's website, https://www.pcr.uu.se/research/ucdp/about-ucdp/. The results yield a slightly different number of clusters, but the salient features of the clusters remain the same.
4. Data can be found at UNHCR (2019).
5. More information on UNHCR data can be found at UNHCR (2013).
6. For a detailed description of the data, refer to UNODC (2019).
7. Data were retrieved from the following sources:
   Republic of Yemen, *World Statesmen.org*, database, http://www.worldstatesmen.org/Yemen.html;
   West Bank and Gaza, *World Statesmen.org*, http://www.worldstatesmen.org/Palestinian_National _Authority.htm;
   South Sudan, *World Statesmen.org*, http://www.worldstatesmen.org/South_Sudan.html;

Timor-Leste, *Encyclopedia.com*, https://www.encyclopedia.com/places/asia/indonesian-political -geography/east-timor#ETHNIC_GROUPS;

Kosovo, Selck and Baghdasaryan (2016);

Serbia, *Wikipedia*, https://en.wikipedia.org/wiki/Serbia#Demographics.

References

Alesina, A., A. Devleeschauwer, W. Easterly, S. Kurlat, and R. Wacziarg. 2003. "Fractionalization." *Journal of Economic Growth* 8 (2): 155–94.

Kaufmann, D., A. Kraay, and M. Mastruzzi. 2011. "The Worldwide Governance Indicators: Methodology and Analytical Issues." *Hague Journal on the Rule of Law* 3 (2): 220–46.

Lange, G. M., Q. Wodon, and K. Carey, eds. 2018. *The Changing Wealth of Nations 2018: Building a Sustainable Future*. Washington, DC: World Bank.

Selck, Torsten J., and Lilit Baghdasaryan. 2016. "Fractionalization of Unrecognized States in Europe." *Wisdom* 6 (1): 1–6. http://www.wisdomperiodical.com/index.php/wisdom/article /download/69/115/.

UNHCR (United Nations High Commissioner for Refugees). 2013. UNHCR Statistical Online Population Database: Sources, Methods and Data Considerations. Database. Geneva: UNHCR. https://www.unhcr.org/statistics/STATISTICS/45c06c662.html#refugees.

UNHCR (United Nations High Commissioner for Refugees). 2019. "Figures at a Glance." Update June 2019. Geneva: UNHCR. https://www.unhcr.org/en-us/figures-at-a-glance.html.

UNODC (United Nations Office on Drugs and Crime). 2019. *Global Study on Homicide*. New York: UNODC. https://www.unodc.org/documents/data-and-analysis/gsh/Booklet1.pdf.

WDI (World Development Indicators). 2017. Database. "Total Natural Resources Rents (% of GDP)." Washington, DC: World Bank. https://data.worldbank.org/indicator/NY.GDP.TOTL.RT.ZS.

Appendix E: Governance Index

A governance index is used as a criterion to rank the clusters obtained in chapter 4. The World Governance Indicators for any given year are highly correlated to one another. Kaufman, Kraay, and Mastruzzi (2011) note how the indicators are strongly and positively correlated across countries. For this reason, we chose not to include the last three indicators in the clustering exercise.

The index is obtained by principal components analysis (PCA), which is a statistical technique commonly used to construct indices.[1] The basic idea is that it extracts from the set of variables a linear combination that captures the largest amount of information common among all variables (Filmer and Pritchett 2001, 116).

The index is estimated for all 203 economies that had governance indicators for 2018. The governance index consists of the first principal component, which explains 84.2 percent of the variation. Every variable included in the index has a Keyser Meyer Olkin (KMO) measure above 0.8, suggesting that all indicators are well suited for the analysis (table E.1).

TABLE E.1 Details about the Governance Index

Component	Eigenvalue	Difference	Proportion	Cumulative
1	5.05448	4.64186	0.8424	0.8424
2	0.412629	0.10461	0.0688	0.9112
3	0.308019	0.175091	0.0513	0.9625
4	0.132928	0.08006	0.0222	0.9847
5	0.0528682	0.013797	0.0088	0.9935
6	0.0390712	n.a.	0.0065	1
No. observations	203			
Trace	6			
Fraction of explained variance	0.9112			

(Table continues on the following page.)

Variable	KMO
Voice and accountability	0.8922
Political stability and absence of violence/terrorism	0.9065
Government effectiveness	0.8387
Regulatory quality	0.8115
Rule of law	0.8751
Control of corruption	0.8725
Overall	0.8625

Note: The difference column notes the difference between one component and the next. Because there is no component 7, there is no difference noted for component 6. KMO = Keyser Meyer Olkin measure; n.a. = not applicable.

The index's sole use is for ranking the clusters in terms of their median governance index.

Note

1. For a detailed discussion on PCA see Lindeman, Merenda, and Gold (1980). An additional source with an application to wealth is Filmer and Pritchett (2001).

References

Filmer, D., and L. H. Pritchett. 2001. "Estimating Wealth Effects without Expenditure Data—or Tears: An Application to Educational Enrollments in States of India." *Demography* 38 (1): 115–32.

Kaufmann, D., A. Kraay, and M. Mastruzzi. 2011. "The Worldwide Governance Indicators: Methodology and Analytical Issues." *Hague Journal on the Rule of Law* 3 (2): 220–46.

Lindeman, R. H., P. F. Merenda, and R. Z. Gold. 1980. *Introduction to Bivariate and Multivariate Analysis.* Glenview, IL: Scott, Foresman.